"*When Friends Ask for Help* is just what is needed for those reluctant counselors who nevertheless find themselves asked for advice from their friends. Dr. Sala has put within reach of the nonprofessional a valuable tool which is simple, yet not simplistic, condensed, yet covering the essentials of counseling from a biblical perspective. It will encourage anyone who wants to help those with problems to give them that which will help them most—sound counsel from the Word of God."

ROSEMARY JENSEN, executive director
Bible Study Fellowship

"The need for quality counseling is becoming overwhelming as personal problems are multiplying in the lives of Christians. . . . Harold Sala helps us to help our fellow Christians with this timely message."

DR. D. ROSS CAMPBELL,
psychiatrist and author

". . .a concise, easy to read, well documented treatment of Biblical and Christian counseling. Anyone interested in helping people with emotional problems will find Dr. Sala's *When Friends Ask for Help* a guide and continuing resource to which he will turn again and again."

DR. JACK MORRIS,
pastor and psychotherapist

"*When Friends Ask for Help* is an excellent synthesis of counseling wisdom for anybody who wants to be a true friend. Although it is written for the lay person, it contains sound advice for professionals as well. Dr. Sala distills t̶ʰ̶ᵉ̶ ̶ᵉˢˢᵉⁿᶜᵉ ̶ᵒᶠ̶ ̶ᴮⁱᵇˡⁱᶜᵃˡ̶ ̶ᵗᵉᵃᶜʰⁱⁿᵍ̶ into a format that res̶   ̶ today."

̶NEY, PH.D.,
psychologist

D0448687

WHEN FRIENDS ASK FOR HELP

BIBLICAL ADVICE ON COUNSELING FRIENDS IN NEED

HAROLD J. SALA, PH. D.

with appendix by psychiatrist
DWIGHT L. CARLSON, M.D.
author of *When Life Isn't Fair*

BARBOUR
PUBLISHING, INC.
Uhrichsville, Ohio

Published by Barbour Publishing, Inc., P. O. Box 719, Uhrichsville,
Ohio 44683 http://www.barbourbooks.com

Cover illustration: Digital imagery® copyright 1999 PhotoDisc, Inc.

Member of the
Evangelical Christian
Publishers Association

Printed in the United States of America.

DEDICATION

To my wonderful wife, Darlene,
who has been my closest friend
and the best counselor I ever had

CONTENTS

PREFACE

More advice is given by friends than by all the psychiatrists, psychologists, and counselors put together. And why not? Who is in a better position to give advice than a friend? After all, whose idiosyncrasies, temperaments, strengths, weaknesses, abilities, and even failures do you know better than your friends'? Besides, we're all more apt to take advice from a friend than we are to consider going for professional counseling.

That's why I wrote this book. It's for all of you who have had little, if any, training in counseling or therapy, yet find yourselves helping other people work through personal problems. You are laypeople who work with others as Bible study leaders, Sunday school teachers, fellowship leaders, teachers, deacons, and church officers. People with problems seem to feel that they will be helped by talking things over with you.

This book is not technical but easy to understand, practical, and scriptural. After all, most of what Jesus said was communicated with nontechnical language, and He was readily understood.

You have probably never thought of yourself as someone who could make a significant contribution to the lives of other people—yet when you stop and think of the conversations you've had with friends and acquaintances, you'll recognize that you've dispensed a lot of advice and support. This book will help you do a better job helping people work through their problems.

The names of individuals I have described have been changed to protect their identities, but the situations about which I have written happened to real people who faced intense, personal problems.

My special thanks to Dr. Vernon Grounds—a friend and mentor for many years—who long ago challenged me to reach out and touch the lives of hurting men and women. I also want to thank Luisa Ampil and Jane LaVau for typing the manuscript and Susan Schlabach of Barbour Publishing for making this book possible. Last of all, I am grateful to my wife, Darlene, and my daughter, Bonnie Craddick, both of whom gave me sound counsel from a woman's perspective.

HAROLD J. SALA
Mission Viejo, California

I welcome your comments and questions. You can write to me at the following address:

DR. HAROLD J. SALA
Guidelines International
Box G
Laguna Hills, CA 92654
E-mail: guidelines@guidelines.org

Chapter 1

You Can Help People!

"What do you think I should do?"

How often have you been asked this question as you have a cup of coffee with a friend—or as you stood chatting with a friend in the parking lot after a meeting?

"Well, what *do* you think I should do?" *You're on, friend.*

You may not be a trained counselor. You may have never taken a night class in counseling or psychology. You may never even have thought of yourself as someone who could significantly help anyone else, yet as soon as you say, "Ah, well, here's what I think. . . ," you are giving counsel. God has opened a door for you to help someone. You are in a position to be used as a channel of divine guidance, to be used in a way that you had never considered possible.

We naturally seek the advice and counsel of those who know us and are closest to us. After all, we are comfortable with our peers and can easily relate to them. We are not embarrassed to talk with them about intimate and personal needs, especially when we are relatively sure they already comprehend what we are facing. With friends, we are not intimidated by the stigma that is often attached to making appointments and going to an office for help.

I am convinced that you do not have to be a psychologist or a clinically trained psychoanalyst to help people. You do not have to be able to interpret dreams or read inkblots or recognize profound psychological insights. Most of the counseling dispensed today is given out by people who have had little training, if any, when it comes to psychology.

In reaction to Freudian or humanistic psychology, some Christians have taken a negative position against psychology and counseling in general. Instead, they should have opposed those forms of counseling that violate scriptural principles. Giving advice or counsel is not the problem; the problem is giving the wrong kind of counsel. Unfortunately, some Christians have tended to throw out the baby with the bath water.

I have heard people say, "I don't believe in counseling—just preaching and praying!" But whenever someone says, "I think you should. . . ," suggesting a course of action to a friend, that person is acting as a counselor. What is more, the "anticounseling" mentality also fails to recognize that Christ's healing ministry was the purest psychiatry ever applied to the emotional wounds of hurting men and women.

When I was in college, the founder of the Christian university I attended reflected a bias of his generation when he said, "Boys [meaning ministerial students], you don't need courses in counseling. All you need is common sense!" An oversimplification? Yes! Especially since common sense isn't so common anymore!

If we called counseling by some other name— say, discipling or ministering—perhaps it would be more acceptable to some. Paul wrote that we who believe in Jesus Christ have been given "the ministry of reconciliation," which means we bring men and women back into harmony both with our heavenly Father and with each other (see 2 Corinthians 5:18–19). Helping to heal broken relationships is one of the most significant contributions you can ever make.

You Have a Mandate to Help People

Writing to the Galatians, Paul instructed, "Brothers, if someone is caught in a sin, you who are spiritual should restore him gently" (Galatians 6:1 NIV). The word Paul used for sin, *paraptoma*, means "false step, transgression."[1] In the context of life today, it means a wrong decision, a poor choice, a relationship that is bound to end in disharmony and suffering. It's a strong word. But the action required to help save a person from sin's fate is both gentle and firm; only those who really care are willing to risk helping another. But if we hope to be truly spiritual, we cannot turn our backs on those who have sinned.

People ask that question—"What do you think

I should do?"—for a variety of reasons. At times they are simply seeking validation for what they really *want* to do and probably will do anyway, no matter what you say. But more often than not the question is asked when a person is uncertain and searching.

Who am I to tell someone else what to do? you might be wondering.

Long ago the psalmist wrote, "The godly man is a good counselor because he is just and fair and knows right from wrong" (Psalm 37:30–31 TLB). Who are you to tell someone else what to do? You are a child of God who is planted on the Rock, Christ Jesus! You don't have to be a Mother Teresa or Billy Graham. God can use your objective perspective to help your friend.

When I was living in the Philippines, whenever I lost my way, I would stop and ask directions. I quickly learned that in the Philippines saying, "I don't know!" made people "lose face." Consequently, when directions were vague and uncertain, I needed to say, "Thank you very much!" and find someone else to ask. But when someone said, "You have to turn around and go back one mile to the first major intersection and take a hard left turn," I knew that I could follow that person's counsel.

When people ask, "What do you think I should do?" often their own judgment has become clouded. Their decision-making abilities are obscured by issues that make it hard for them to see the consequences of their actions. If your thinking is clear, you become an asset of immeasurable value. You can give directions to others who are lost and confused.

As part of the family of God, we have a responsibility to each other. A family is a series of interlocking relationships, and the quality of the relationships affects the quality of family living. We're like a team of mountain climbers linked together by rope; when one stumbles or falls, another can be the anchor that holds steady.

Once when my son was climbing mountains in Switzerland, he noticed three climbers on the face of another incline. Suddenly, one lost his footing and fell. The second man was supposed to be his anchor, but that man fell under the weight of the first; then the two of them pulled the third loose. The three tumbled hundreds of feet down the face of the glacier. (Fortunately they were able to walk away from the fall.)

That's often the way it is when someone makes a bad decision. "It's my life, and I can do with it what I please!" The one who says that seldom sees the consequences of his or her actions in relationship to the rest of the family members or friends, linked together by the bonds of love forged over the years.

The Bible stresses that we have a responsibility to help our Christian brothers and sisters make good decisions. At least fifty-eight times, we find "one another" phrases in the New Testament, all expressing some kind of obligation or responsibility we have to each other in the body of Christ. Among the many, you will find that we should:

- love one another
- pray for one another
- bear one another's burden
- encourage one another
- exhort one another
- admonish one another

When we obey these instructions, we become counselors.

In swampy areas of the world, a geological condition can develop that is called "quicksand." An unsuspecting animal or person who happens to step into this sandy mire is sucked deeper and deeper; unless the person or animal is rescued, loss of life is certain.

No one in his right mind would ever intentionally walk into quicksand, right? But once the person is sinking, he needs help to get himself out of that situation. That's the way it is with our problems. The person who asks, "What should I do?" may feel absolutely overwhelmed. He feels the downward pull of a situation that seems hopeless.

That's where you come into the picture. You're not caught in the quicksand; you're still standing on solid ground. Consequently, you have the responsibility to say, "I think you should. . ." If we avoid our responsibilities to our brothers and sisters simply because we don't consider ourselves "professionals," we walk away from hurting people who could have so easily been helped.

Helping people through counseling is part of what Paul urged the Galatians to do when he told them to bear each other's burdens and thus fulfill the great law of love (see Galatians 6:1–5). We are all responsible for each other. If we fail to meet this responsibility, we create a vacuum in the Christian community that altogether too often is filled by unsaved men and women whose counseling techniques may violate the principles of God's Word.

If you still are not convinced that you can help people, allow me to point out two very important facts: (1) You have at your disposal the solid direction of the Word of God, a "lamp to [our] feet and a light to [our] path" (Psalm 119:105); and (2) God's Holy Spirit indwells you as His child, and He can give you insight and wisdom far beyond your human capacity (see Romans 8:9). If you know Jesus Christ as your personal Lord and Savior, you have an anchor that lets you throw a lifeline to people being sucked down by life's quicksand.

Let's take a look at the way counseling in this framework of Christian faith enables you to be effective as a people-helper.

COUNSELING WITHIN A BIBLICAL FRAMEWORK

Recently, I spent a month in the beautiful little country of New Zealand, and during that time I drove an automobile very much like the one I drive at home. Like my own car, it had four wheels, a horn, and a steering wheel.

Driving was different, however. New Zealanders drive on the left side of the road (no, not necessarily the *wrong* side). I had to convert my thinking: *Pull to the left instead of the right.* I had to keep telling myself, *Watch for cars passing on the right!* I never would have arrived at my destination without re-adjusting my thinking as well as my driving.

In the same way, when you counsel from faith's perspective, you need to convert your thinking; you have to make a conscious effort to leave behind the world's philosophy and instead align your thoughts with the gospel. Paul told the Corinthians, whose culture and society was sensual and worldly, if a person is in Christ, he or she is a different person; everything becomes new (see 2 Corinthians 5:17).

Counseling from a biblical perspective doesn't mix the profane and the godly (like a man who drives on the left side of the road for a while and then switches over to the other side so he can see the scenery better). The person who counsels within the gospel's framework makes a commitment; he goes God's way no matter what others think.

In some Christian circles today, many people are weaving back and forth. They follow humanistic principles, advocating and endorsing lifestyles that clearly don't meet with God's approval. When they counsel others, they work with secular models; they conform their advice to the teaching of people whose lives are totally out of harmony with Scripture. These counselors may sprinkle a few Bible verses here and there throughout their counseling, as if to sanctify a pagan system, but they fail to follow the Bible's clear directions on life. God's approach to dealing with our needs is vastly different from human methods.

How does counseling within a biblical framework differ from secular counseling? What presuppositions do you adopt if you are committed to Christ?

Counseling from a Biblical Perspective Recognizes the Authority of God's Word, the Bible

Once we recognize that the Bible is God's "psychiatry," much of our lives' confusion disappears.

Right here I need to say something that will help you help other people. If God is a good God—and I am convinced that He is—then His direction is also good. The person who asks you, "What do you think I should do?" may not like the counsel you give (counsel you feel is consistent with Scripture's guidelines and principles), but if that person accepts the authority of God's Word, you can give clear direction. When your counsel is based on Scripture, you need not doubt its wisdom. In secular counseling, however, a cacophony of voices competes for dominance, and none of them resonates with certainty.

For example, in one experiment Professor D. L. Rosenhan planted eight sane volunteers, one of them a psychiatrist, in eight different psychiatric wards and told them to behave normally. Many inmates immediately recognized that these eight were impostors because their behavior was rational and their conversations meaningful, yet not one staff psychiatrist recognized the symptom of normalcy. Said Professor Rosenhan, "Any diagnostic process that lends itself so readily to massive errors of this sort cannot be a very reliable one."[2]

Secular psychoanalysis, which follows the framework first advocated by Sigmund Freud, takes on the average six to eight years, and even then it is only partially effective. One-third of all patients undergoing psychoanalysis are eventually "cured," one-third are helped somewhat, and one-third are not helped at all—the same ratio of "cure" in people who receive no professional help whatsoever.[3]

However, I want to make very clear that I have no ax to grind with modern psychiatry, but only with those treatments and philosophies that contradict the counsel of God's Word, the Bible. Our word "psychiatry" comes from two Greek words: *psyche* (soul) and *iatra* (healing). It literally means "healing of the soul." Obviously, God is in favor of psychiatry; He wants our souls to be whole and healthy. But the bottom line is this: What God says in His Word is our only source for true and eternal soul healing.

Today a growing number of psychiatrists are

committed to the principles of the Word at the same time they use psychiatry as a tool for healing. Psychiatrists like Dr. Ross Campbell of the Southeastern Counseling Center in Chattanooga, Tennessee, and Dr. Paul Meier of the Minirth-Meier Clinic in Dallas have not simply "sprinkled a few verses" over a secular counseling model. Instead, they are committed without reservation to the authority of Scripture.

The person who accepts the Word's authority believes that it was given by the inspiration of the Holy Spirit; the Bible is not simply one of many different options that may work. It is *the way* to fulfillment and happiness. However, having counseled and worked with people for more than thirty years, I have come to the conclusion that even if I were not a Christian and did not believe that I was ultimately accountable to God, I would still give the same counsel and direction. I am convinced the guidelines we find in God's Word are necessary for people to live well-adjusted lives with meaning and purpose.

The Bible recognizes that our fundamental problem is estrangement from our Creator: "sin." This old-fashioned and seldom-used word is rarely found in the vocabulary of secular psychiatry. Some psychiatrists, however, have addressed the issue of sin. Psychiatrist Karl Menninger of the famed Menninger Clinic wrote this in *Whatever Became of Sin?:*

> *I believe there is "sin" which is expressed in ways which cannot be subsumed under verbal*

*artifacts such as "crime," "disease," "delin-
quency," "deviancy." There is immorality; there
is unethical behavior; there is wrongdoing.
And I hope to show that there is usefulness in
retaining that concept, and indeed the word,
sin, which now shows some signs of returning
to public acceptance. I would like to help this
trend along.*[4]

Dealing with our estrangement from God and
each other is a fundamental issue that the Bible ad-
dresses clearly. Critics of the Bible, charging that
religion creates guilt by making people *feel* guilty, fail
to recognize that the cross of Jesus Christ provides
redemption and forgiveness, thus eliminating the
burden of human failure. Long ago, Augustine said,
"Thou hast made us for Thyself, O God, and our
heart is restless until it finds its rest in Thee."

The Bible Is a Guide for Moral Conduct

Some think of the Scripture's counsel as an impossible dream, something well and good, lofty and noble
—but just not practical in our world today. Others
think of it as a benchmark, something to strive for—
but unrealistic and impossible to attain. I recognize
that the lives of many people fall far short of the
Scripture's standard, but that is not God's fault. He
has not demanded the impossible of us; rather, we

have failed to attain the measure of happiness that He wants for us. As G. K. Chesterton once said, "Christianity has not been tried and found lacking; it has been tried and found difficult."

Once, I had just spoken on commitment in marriage, when an attractive, nicely dressed, middle-aged woman approached me and said, "About your message this morning. . ." She paused, then flushed and said, "I tried it. . .but it didn't work!"

Somewhat surprised by her bluntness, I said, "You tried what?"

"Well, I tried to live by the Bible and it just didn't work!"

The Scripture's counsel works only if you cooperate with God, striving to do what He wants you to do. You are not a machine that mechanically does only the will of its inventor; you are a person made in the image of God, with will, intelligence, and emotions. Most importantly, you were given the tremendous power of choice; your decisions make the difference as you create your future.

God says, "This is the way to happiness. Walk this path." With that direction comes the power of the Holy Spirit, enabling you to rise above the quicksand of your old sinful nature. The old cry of, "I can't help the way I am," is drowned out by the chorus of those who can say through experience, "I'm a different person because Christ changed my life and put my feet on the solid Rock."

When you help a friend by counseling from a

biblical perspective, your approach is this: God said what He meant and meant what He said. He neither excuses nor condones our sin or failure, but He extends forgiveness and helps overcome the pull of our old natures. Our loving God wants only good for His children.

The Bible Is Countercultural

We live in a pagan society that constantly bombards us with ideas, attitudes, suggestions, and lifestyles that are out of harmony with God's great plan. The person who struggles with decisions affecting her future may be strongly pulled by two forces: the flesh and her culture.

The flesh—or the old selfish nature—often pulls her away from the path of God's will. Remember Paul's struggle with this as he cried out, "For the good that I will to do, I do not do; but the evil I will not to do, that I practice" (Romans 7:19).

Our culture is the fabric that surrounds our lives, and it's reinforced by the media, our heroes and heroines. We come face-to-face with our culture when we wait at the checkout counter in the grocery store, wishing we could look like the beautiful people on the magazine covers.

Let's see how the flesh and our culture affect a real-life situation. Suppose you have a friend, Lois. She's a single woman with a good sales position in a growing company. Her boss, John, invites her to attend a convention with him in Las Vegas and immediately she says, "Great idea!" She is ready for a little excitement and a change of scenery, but then he tells her to make reservations—one room with a double bed. Lois doesn't say anything, but she's troubled.

The boss's secretary says, "Way to work up the corporate ladder!"

Someone else tells her, "What difference does it make? Everybody does it these days as long as it's safe."

But Lois is a Christian, a single mother who longs for a good husband who could also be a father to her two little boys. Thinking about the weekend and the sexual expectations that go with it, her conscience says, *Hey, you don't want to get tangled up in this. You know it's wrong! This is not for you!* But when she talks to you about the situation, she admits that she feels attracted to her boss. After all, he's witty, intelligent, and fun; and he makes her feel important, something her ex-husband never did.

That's the pull of her flesh, her old selfish nature. The "who cares?" attitude of her coworkers is her culture. The will of God opposes them both.

God's counsel runs contrary to our old natures and the culture in which we live. That's something you must bear in mind when you counsel from the perspective of God's Word.

That's quite a claim! you may be saying to yourself. Yet if God's will is not broad enough to give us guidance in all the decisions and choices of life, including the ones that have recently been created by science, culture, and medicine, then God would have left us vulnerable to some of the most pressing and crucial issues confronting men and women today. God will not leave us in darkness or leave us on our own when it comes to the issues of life. Remember the promise of Jesus: "I am the light of the world. He who follows Me shall not walk in darkness, but have the light of life" (John 8:12).

The Bible gives pointed statements indicating His will when it comes to most of today's issues. For example:

> The kind of person you should marry
> (see 2 Corinthians 6:14)

> Your moral life outside of marriage
> (see 1 Thessalonians 4:3)

> The way you conduct your business
> (see Romans 12)

> Why you should keep your marriage
> together (see 1 Peter 3:7)

The references I've just listed are clear and unequivocal. You may not like what God says, but you can understand clearly what He wants.

Still, many issues are unique to our times. They weren't even thought of when Paul wrote the Epistles, but God has not ignored these situations; He gives us guidance through biblical principles. These principles apply to such issues as abortion, surrogate mothering, in vitro fertilization, test-tube babies, euthanasia, and so on.

Whether or not God ever intended us to be confronted with some of those issues is not the question; we *are* faced with them. At some point we have to say, "Yes, I believe this is pleasing to God!" or "No way! I don't think God would approve of this because of the principles we find in Scripture!"

If you look in a concordance under "A," you will not find the word *abortion*—but as you search the pages of Scripture, you will find statements like, "For you created my inmost being; you knit me together in my mother's womb. . . . When I was woven together in the depths of the earth, your eyes saw my unformed body. All the days ordained for me were written in your book before one of them came to be" (Psalm 139:13, 15–16 NIV).

From this you can synthesize a principle: Life is a gift from God; it is sacred. And this principle gives you personal guidance in the choices that confront you.

All Genuine Healing Comes from God

A fundamental premise of Scripture is that sin separates men and women from God and from each other —but healing produces restoration and harmony. Scriptural redemption involves healing—spiritually, emotionally, and yes, even physically. God said through Moses, "I am the LORD who heals you" (Exodus 15:26). Through David we learn that God "forgives all [our] sins and heals all [our] diseases" (Psalm 103:3 NIV). Jesus went about healing "many who were sick with various diseases" (Mark 1:34). "Wherever He entered, into villages, cities, or the country," reported Mark, "they laid the sick in the marketplaces, and begged Him that they might just touch the hem of His garment. And as many as touched Him were made well" (Mark 6:56). Counseling from a biblical perspective is an extension of Christ's healing ministry. This ministry reaches into the realm of the emotions and the spirit.

For you to be an effective counselor and helper of hurting people, however, there is one more important prerequisite.

Counseling from a Biblical Perspective
Requires a Working Knowledge
of God's Word

"But I am just a layperson!"

"Why not just refer people to our pastor? After

all, isn't that what we pay him for?"

"I've never gone to Bible school or a (college!"

"I can't help anybody!"

You don't have to use these excuses. The chapters that follow will give you a plan that does work. It is simple. Like the Four Spiritual Laws, which have helped thousands to share their faith, the formula I have developed for laypeople takes the sweat out of helping people. It works with personal problems, family problems, even business problems.

But before you can really be effective in helping people, you need to know what the Word says about some of the fundamental issues of life:

- roles, relationships, and responsibilities in family living
- sin and guilt
- forgiveness and restitution
- fear—and the faith that overcomes it
- the place of sex in our lives and marriage

Jay Adams, in his book *Competent to Counsel,* a valued source book for serious Christian counselors, contends that the best possible preparation for counseling is a seminary education. This, however, is impossible for most of you reading this book. Don't be overwhelmed by your own inadequacy. You have another choice: Find out what the Bible says about these key issues. Become a "lay specialist."

By the time you finish this book, you will have

been exposed to what the Word says about the basic issues people face. That knowledge will give you confidence when you hear the question, "What do you think I should do?" You will have some idea how to answer, using God's plan for wholeness in relationships and lives.

Go deeper on your own by marking in your Bible the passages used in this study. Make your own cross-references in the margin of your Bible; where you know a Scripture verse on a given topic, make a note of another verse that relates to the same issue. Use the blank pages at the end of your Bible. This will be your handbook when someone asks for help in working through an issue. I'll also give you some techniques that will help you be more effective.

The formula you will be using is this:

$$\boxed{\begin{array}{c} \text{THE} \\ \text{WORD} \end{array}} + \boxed{\begin{array}{c} \text{COUNSELING} \\ \text{TECHNIQUES} \end{array}} = \boxed{\begin{array}{c} \text{GOD'S} \\ \text{PSYCHIATRY} \end{array}}$$

Now, let's take the first step: getting started.

QUESTIONS FOR THOUGHT AND DISCUSSION

1. Why do you think Christians have often not been receptive to psychology and counseling?

2. In your own words, explain what Paul meant by a "ministry of reconciliation" (2 Corinthians 5:18–19). How do you think this relates to lay counseling?

3. If Christians were following the Bible's commands to love, support, and help one another, do you think psychology would be the booming business it is today? Why or why not?

4. Why does Dr. Sala believe the Bible is "God's psychiatry"? How does this perspective change the way you think about God's Word?

5. List a few of today's controversial issues. Then find Bible references that offer principles applicable to each.

Chapter 2

Getting Started

Today we live in a world of quick fixes, fast foods, and instant replay. We aren't content with waiting for answers tomorrow; we want everything today, right now. A sign in a restaurant reads, "Lord bless the instant coffee, the one-minute oatmeal, and the pop-up waffles. In haste, Amen!" When it comes to unraveling difficulties, most folks also want immediate, painless solutions. And of course, these do not usually exist. So don't expect to be able to dispense successful one-minute answers to a person's problems. Counseling takes time and effort.

The person who has turned to you for help is probably at a fork in the road of life. The decision he makes may have consequences that go far into the future. Though you hardly need to be concerned about legal implications (unless you counsel professionally or accept money in payment for counseling), you do assume a measure of responsibility for that person's future.

Whenever you say, "I think you should. . . ," you are potentially the catalyst for a change in the entire direction of a friend's life. Dispensing free advice is a serious matter. What you say may keep a friend's marriage together; it may send someone in the direction of a new career; it may even make the difference between life and death for someone who has lost her way.

In the previous chapter, I pointed out that we bear a responsibility before God for each other as part of His family; we are to help, guide, and encourage one another. Jesus told the disciples that after He had returned to heaven they would carry on His works and do even greater things than He had. His words must have been intimidating to the disciples; nonetheless, they were true.

Today the healing, restoring, and helping ministry of Jesus is done through us, His people, His body. That knowledge should not only make you want to better equip and train yourself for helping people; it should also make you more willing to make the sacrifices and take the risks involved with helping someone else.

Helping People Takes Time

Visualize a case of empty soft drink bottles sitting on your back patio as you water the flowers in your garden. The spray from the hose falls across the small openings of the bottles. A tiny amount of water finds its way into the individual containers. Not much, but some. Now, in contrast, visualize taking a bucket of water, and then filling each bottle, one at a time, with a dipper. Takes a lot longer than just spraying the bottles with the hose, right? But the results are much different. That's the difference between someone listening to a pastor's sermon or a Bible study with two hundred people present—and going one-on-one with a friend.

In tennis, when someone serves a ball into your court, it's up to you. You may backhand it, use your forehand, smash a volley as hard as you can, or drop an easy shot over the net, but once the ball is in your court, it's your move. You can't fold your arms and wait for someone else to take care of it.

When someone finally gets around to that question, "What do you think I should do?" the ball is in your court. If you are really serious about wanting to help, you have to be willing to make a commitment of time and emotional energy. You have to be willing to be involved in the life of that person. You can't fold your arms and wait for the pastor or someone else to get involved.

You can, of course, ignore the question and not respond. But the person wouldn't have asked unless he was serious about wanting your input. Suppose he already has a course of action he's considering. If you fail to respond, that tends to endorse what he's already thinking. Since you didn't offer any alternatives, he assumes that you are in agreement. That can be dangerous.

A pastor came to me and poured out his heart. I listened. I didn't agree with him or his assessment of the situation, but I didn't say so, thinking that we'd talk about it another time. Later, I had an irate call from one of the deacons in his church. He had heard I had supported the pastor in their dispute.

"Hold on!" I said. "Who said I agreed with him?"

"The pastor!"

My mistake was that I had listened and didn't respond; the pastor had interpreted that as my tacit endorsement.

If you fail to follow through when you are asked for help, you may also end up causing even more damage. If you do not have the time to help someone, or you feel the better part of discretion would be to let someone else help (a perfectly appropriate decision in some cases) because you simply are not qualified, you still need to do something to get the ball across the court. You can't just walk away and leave it sitting there.

Often all you need to do is take an hour or even two to talk through a situation over a cup of coffee. During that time you can reinforce the voice of conscience with enough fiber that the person can make the right decision. For instance, in the previous chapter I told about Lois, the young woman who was invited to the convention in Las Vegas; as the result of sharing her heart with a friend, she had the courage to go back and say, "I made reservations for *two* rooms. I can do a better job for our company when I'm not emotionally involved!"

Often, though, it takes more than one cup of coffee to work through a problem. If your schedule doesn't allow you the time to be involved, you may need to say something like, "Look, I care about you, and I sense that this is something really important to you, but it's going to take some time to work through this. I've got to be out of town for the next three weekends, and I think this is too important to wait until I get back. Why don't you talk with [someone you can recommend]?" That way you've gotten the ball out of your court.

Most of the time, though, we sell short ourselves and our abilities to help other people. I am convinced that you are far more able to be a positive force for good in the lives of others than you think. I believe this book will give you new insights and tools to help you.

GUIDELINES FOR EFFECTIVE COUNSELING

The following guidelines are not profound. You might be tempted to think, *Anybody would know that!* They are simple basics, fundamentals that must be observed. Failing to follow through with them hurts our chances of really helping someone.

As I write this, major league baseball teams are heading for spring training. They are the pros that keep on thrilling baseball fans, yet every spring training the coaches emphasize the same fundamentals: batting, catching, sliding, and timing. Too simple? No, simply necessary.

When You are Asked,
"What Do You Think I Should Do?"
Reserve Your Comment until You Are
Certain You Have the Complete Picture

The greatest single failure of untrained individuals is jumping to conclusions. You say things such as, "Well, it's obvious to me what your problem is. . ." Or you mentally thumb through your memorized roster of Bible verses, select a couple that seem to have enough weight, and then bang! You hit 'em between the eyes with both of them.

Suppose you say, "Lois, I'm really surprised at you. How would you even consider spending the weekend in Vegas with the jerk you work for? You've got two kids, and, besides, you teach Sunday school. You know better than that!"

What Lois really needs to know is how to handle the situation. She isn't so much interested in going to bed with the guy (she wouldn't have to go to a convention to do that) as she is in knowing how to respond without offending him while preserving her integrity. She doesn't need your shocked disapproval.

When you come down hard on someone without understanding the situation, you frustrate and even anger the person who has come to you for help. You'll never hear those words, "What do you think I should do?" from that person again! Simplistic solutions to complex issues offer no real help.

Quite often, when a person comes to me for

help, I get the feeling that the person is testing or proving me. The person is sizing me up, thinking, *Can this guy really help me? Should I really unload on him?* We'll often talk about trivia, then a surface problem, and finally, *WHAM!* she lets me have it. The real problem! Had I jumped to a premature conclusion, I would never have had the privilege of helping her work through the real issue. She needed time before she could trust me enough to talk about her root problems.

Often these deep issues are intimate and sensitive. Most people are embarrassed to expose their real difficulties until you have established a trust that's built on an atmosphere of safety and acceptance.

Be Principled as You Handle Confidences

Nothing will hurt a friendship or destroy your credibility faster than breaking confidence with people. It adds insult to injury and bitterness to sorrow. Take, for example, the woman who wrote me about a son in his early twenties who announced that he was gay. The mother went to the pastor of their church and unburdened her heart, telling him the entire story.

The next Sunday, however, the pastor related the whole story in his morning message. He didn't use the boy's name; he didn't have to. The church was fairly small, and the boy's identity was obvious. The mother said, "That has been our home church for more than twenty years, but right now I'd rather take a beating than go there!"

What do you do, though, when someone shares something that has explosive consequences? Suppose a teenager is running away from home, a discouraged business colleague is going to take his life, an acquaintance is ripping off the company for which he works; what should you do then? Let me give you a clear guideline:

When a person's life is endangered or the consequences of somebody's actions violate the law or seriously affect the lives of other people, you have no alternative but to bring someone else into the picture.

What I recommend is that you convince the person that you care, you are a friend, and you love the person so much that you will stand with him through this whole situation. Then show him that other people are necessary to resolve the problem. If someone admits to you he has broken the law, offer to go with him to the appropriate officials; stand by him while he does what he needs to do to make things right. Or you might accompany a teenager to the doctor to find out if she is really pregnant, and then, when she is convinced that she needs to bring her mother into the situation, go with her to break the news to Mom.

Often, your support will be enough to help someone make the right decision and begin to work through a problem that has been pushed aside for far too long.

Be Patient with People

Habits that have been many years in the making may not be resolved in a matter of a few minutes. At the same time, however, you have the right to expect change, since the Holy Spirit is the greatest agent of behavioral change the world has ever known. Jay Adams says, "Change for some people is difficult to accept. Change is difficult because change means doing something new, something unusual, something not done before. It usually means exchanging old habit patterns for new ones."[1] Growth requires change, and the fact that someone is hurting necessitates change in personal relationships or patterns of behavior. But it takes time.

Be Professional

Yes, I know, you are not a professional counselor, but you can value a relationship with someone so much that you treat with a professional manner the confidence she has placed in you.

Whenever you reach out to a hurting person of the opposite sex, you run the risk of emotional involvement. You can be concerned for people and at the same time keep your emotions firmly in control; however, all too many counselors have gotten into trouble here. They listened to someone pour out the pain of being betrayed by a mate, and then, as the scalding tears came, they reached out with a warm embrace. The high voltage of that emotional situation eventually developed into a relationship that compromised marriages on all sides.

Let's go back to the situation with Lois. She likes John as a person and admires certain characteristics in his life. She also knows that his constant travel doesn't go over very well with his wife, a rather introverted person who is content to stay at home.

Lois's refusal to book a room with a double bed brings a profuse and sincere apology. John assures her that he wasn't making sexual advances. He says that he intended it as a joke; Lois doesn't quite believe that, of course. On the two-hour plane ride, however, John candidly shares some of his frustration with his marriage. Something pathetic in what he says touches the maternal part of Lois's psyche.

She is not the one who should be helping John to work through his personal problems, however; she would be far too apt to become involved herself. After all, she is single and lonely. She's also the personification of what John's wife is not—pretty, nicely dressed, and outgoing.

Some people whose marriages are solid do decide to get emotionally involved in helping members of the opposite sex. Only you can evaluate the dangers. Some folks are "huggers," and embracing someone who is hurting is just as natural as it is for me to take a hand and shake it warmly. I, for one, though, advise a certain caution when it comes to embracing members of the opposite sex who have come to you for help. Their emotions may be volatile, and the person you embrace may wish desperately that a mate would do the same thing. When you embrace someone, your action can trigger an emotional response that is not in the best interests of either of you. A warm handshake, direct eye contact, a hospitable cup of coffee or a Coke are all ways of conveying warmth apart from physical contact.

Never counsel a member of the opposite sex when you question your ability to handle a situation. A prominent pastor was approached for marital counseling by the beautiful wife of one of his deacons. The pastor told her, "Look, you are a beautiful woman and I'm a red-blooded male, and I just don't trust myself to counsel you!" Shocked? Yes, I was when I heard the pastor relate that story, because I know he is a man of God whose ministry is effective. But he knew his weaknesses and openly recognized them.

Most of the time we dispense lay counseling informally, perhaps at the office, riding the commuter train home, after a church meeting, or during a lunch break. After the initial encounter, however, you have some control over the circumstances that follow. You need a quiet place without interruptions or small children, which may mean you say, "Lois, will you have lunch with me on Thursday? I know a place on Thirty-second Street where we can have an hour without the phone ringing."

But it's okay to bring your husband or wife into a counseling situation, especially when you are counseling a member of the opposite sex. For instance, you might say, "You know, my husband has a lot of insights into how guys think and feel. What would you think about joining us for a cup of coffee Friday night and we can all talk about this together?"

For your own sake, guard against counseling someone in a place where your integrity could be called into question (such as in a home with someone of the opposite sex when no one else is present, or in a hotel room). Your willingness to help may be completely honorable, but the circumstances don't make the situation look legitimate. The apostle Paul warned against this in 1 Thessalonians 5:22.

Recognize Your Own Limitations

You never lose the respect of someone when you say, "You know, I'd like to help you with this, but it is more than I can handle. I'd like to suggest that you see. . ." (and make a referral to a counselor or a physician).

Don't play medical doctor, either. It's dangerous as well as unethical. If someone you are working with has made a commitment to Jesus Christ, and that person has been under the care of a medical doctor who has prescribed medication, don't say, "Now that you have found the Lord, you aren't going to need your medicine anymore!"

Sometimes I am absolutely convinced that the person doesn't need the medication which a physician prescribed, but I encourage the friend to go back to the doctor for evaluation. If the friend is under the care of a doctor who is well known for overmedicating his patients, I might recommend another doctor, one who I know will take the time to listen to what the patient says instead of merely writing prescriptions. If you know the doctor personally, you might even want to brief him on what has taken place.

In Bible Study Fellowship, Barbara became a good friend with her discussion leader, a warm-hearted, mature woman who reminded her of her own mother. Joann, the discussion leader, hadn't ever thought of herself as a counselor, but the discussions following the Wednesday studies helped Barbara through a very difficult time in her life when her husband was having an affair with his secretary. But when Barbara started talking about suicide, Joann knew that the situation was beyond her. Joann convinced Barbara that she needed help that she couldn't give. Joann made an appointment for Barbara with a Christian psychologist in their area and went to the office with her (partly to insure that she kept the appointment).

Later, Barbara said it was Joann's friendship, not the counsel of the professional, that really brought her through that difficult time of her life. But had Joann failed to reach for additional help and had

Barbara taken her life, Joann would have carried a tremendous load for the rest of her life.

*Nurture Your Relationship with
the Person You are Helping*

Your effectiveness with the person you want to help is determined to a large degree by the relationship you have with that person. Why did your friend come to you initially? Because you are a "nice person"? You just happened to be there? He feels comfortable with you? Possibly all three. He felt that you could help, even if it was only by extending a sympathetic, listening ear. Often you help another person a great deal by simply listening, something no one else may have done.

When you counsel a friend, your relationship is especially important. Proverbs 27:6 notes, "Faithful are the wounds of a friend." A loyal friend is honest. Words of counsel may hurt and even wound, as the writer of Proverbs attested, but those wounds will heal and may prevent a far greater tragedy.

If you tell someone only what he or she wants to hear, your value as a counselor is diminished; on the other hand, if you are so harsh that you drive the person away, your effectiveness is finished. The person you help needs to know you are honest because you truly care.

If you are counseling a couple, you may strive

to be neutral and objective; yet when issues of right and wrong are at stake, the offending person may feel that you as a counselor have "ganged up" with the offended party. You need to make sure the one you are trying to help feels accepted as a person, even though you may reject his behavior. How do you do this?

Relationships that are built on the foundation of respect, trust, and genuine cordiality form bonds that enable you to keep the lines of communication open when the going gets sticky. Your character and integrity give you status in the eyes of others. Though you may not have thought of yourself in this light, people think of you as "having your act together," meaning they think you can help them get their act together as well.

Before people run the risk of telling you where they are hurting, they usually ask themselves three questions: *Can this person help me? Does this person care about me? Does this person know what he is talking about?*

The last question (a matter of knowledge) doesn't matter as much to most people. Bartenders dispense a lot of advice, but few bartenders have had any training in counseling. They're just willing to listen. If you tend to pontificate or come across as an authority figure who sits in condemnation of the person who turns to you, you're finished. But if people sense you genuinely care about them, they will be more apt to believe you can really help them.

Genuine, warm concern forges lasting relationships that allow you to be an anchor when the storms of life buffet people. The foundation for counseling is done long before you ever hear those words, "What do you think I should do?"

Jesus radiated this kind of warmth to the people who were touched by His life. One of my favorite passages in Scripture is the story found in John 8, when the Pharisees shoved a prostitute before Jesus with the scathing words, "Now Moses, in the law, commanded us that such should be stoned. But what do you say?" At first Jesus ignored their question, but when they kept asking, He raised Himself up and said to them, "He who is without sin among you, let him throw a stone at her first" (verse 7).

Then Jesus leaned over and began writing on the ground (the only record of Jesus' ever writing anything). John doesn't tell us what He wrote, but I've wondered if perhaps He wrote a date on the ground; then He looked up at a man who quickly remembered what he had done on that date and slipped away, fearful that Jesus would tell what he had done. In all probability, the men who seized that girl knew where to find her, because they had been in the same place on unofficial business more than once.

As her detractors left one by one, Jesus said, "Where are those accusers of yours? Has no one condemned you?"

"No one, Lord," she said.

"Neither do I condemn you."

What unqualified acceptance! Then Jesus followed with the words, "Go and sin no more" (John 8:10–11). She knew that Jesus rejected her sin but accepted her as a person.

Some, however, who ask for help are left with the impression that the one to whom they have turned for help is more interested in the lascivious details than in helping them overcome it. We can all learn a lesson from the way Jesus handled the conversation with the fallen woman. He knew exactly where she was coming from, yet He refrained from asking the questions some people would have asked, such as:

- How did you get into this profession?
- How many men do you see every night?
- Do you enjoy what you are doing?

Christ didn't focus on the past but the present ("Where are your accusers?") and the future ("Go and sin no more"). When you counsel someone, the real issue is where does the person go from here and how does she get there?

Rely Totally upon the Lord as You Counsel People

To be a godly counselor and friend you need to pray as you listen. This doesn't mean you close your eyes and bow your head while someone talks to you; but it does mean you keep yourself in an attitude of prayer, silently saying, *Lord, help me to pick up on the silent signals and read the nonverbal cues. Help me to hear what is really being said.*

When your heart is open to Him, the Holy Spirit will often give you intuitive knowledge. As you ask the right questions, the ones the Spirit nudges you to ask, the person you are counseling will begin to reveal the real issue.

Now let's see how it works.

QUESTIONS FOR
THOUGHT AND DISCUSSION

1. Have you ever turned to someone for help, only to be given a pat, self-righteous answer? If so, how did you feel?

2. Why might you hesitate to become a friend's "coffee cup counselor"? Which of your reasons for hesitation are legitimate? Which aren't?

3. What was Jesus' attitude when confronted with sin? Is this different from our own? If so, how?

CHAPTER 3

THE FIRST MEETING

The phone rings and an acquaintance says, "Have you heard about. . . ?" You hadn't, but you get an earful in a few minutes.

"I think you ought to go talk to her about this!" the caller says.

Should you go?

Generally, confrontational counseling is not very successful. When someone "sics" me on a friend, I often explain that there are three things I cannot do: I can't climb a fence that leans toward me, kiss a person who leans away from me, or help someone who doesn't want help. On occasion I have said, "Look, I understand that you want me to help this person, and I'd like to do that. But until she is ready to let me help, I can't do much."

If I hear that a friend is struggling with something, I may arrange for a cup of coffee or lunch, simply to let the person know I am his friend. Spending time together gives the other person an opportunity to open up, without letting him know that I have already been informed of the problem.

When the friend's struggles are public knowledge, you may want to give that person a call and say, "Look, I'm available. If you want to get together and talk, let me know. I'll be there pronto!"

When Do You Drop Everything?
And When Don't You?

Sometimes when the phone rings, you will clearly sense the situation is an emergency that calls for crisis measures. Other times someone may need help, but the situation doesn't call for you to give up your evening at home with your family. In that case, setting a time to meet at your convenience is perfectly appropriate.

Psychologist Clyde Narramore felt strongly about not letting others unnecessarily disturb his time with his family at home. One evening the phone rang, and the caller said, "Dr. Narramore, I've just got to talk to you tonight. My marriage is about to fold."

"How old are you?" inquired Narramore.

The caller answered, "Forty-two."

"How many years have you been married?"

"Seventeen years."

"If you are forty-two years of age and have been married for seventeen years, you'll live until morning," said Dr. Narramore. "I'll be happy to see you at the office at nine o'clock."

Two Sides to Every Story

Most of the time, a husband or wife wants to talk with me alone, but if a couple needs help with their marriage and both are willing to come together, I much prefer talking with them together. Why? That way, each knows what the other has said, and each has an opportunity to clarify the issues.

Unless you hear both sides of the issue, you cannot be certain that the story you are hearing is the true one. Always be aware that your friend can only describe her own perspective. Reality may be something quite different.

Proverbs 18:17 says, "The first to present his case seems right, till another comes forward and questions him" (NIV). Reject the temptation to form a verdict until you hear from both parties. If you cannot hear the other side of the story, at least be aware that it exists. Help your friend grasp the fact that others will view the same events differently.

WHERE TO MEET

Counseling needs to be comfortable and personal. An office tends to be cold and clinical. A living room usually isn't much of an improvement—too formal. Chairs are too far apart, and it's too structured. On the other hand, however, your kitchen is a warm, friendly environment. If you sit at your kitchen table, you will be close to your friend, you can offer a cup of coffee or a soft drink, and you have a surface on which to write should you want to make notes.

If you meet at a restaurant, give some thought to its environment. You need quiet and a measure of privacy. Some restaurants are impossible environments for carrying on meaningful conversations because of the way the tables are placed. By the same token, the hustling "get 'em in and out" restaurant employees do nothing to encourage a confidential conversation.

But as I said, I do find that having a writing surface handy helps me out as a counselor, and a restaurant naturally provides this. I personally like to make a few brief notes for myself as I listen to someone. Sometimes the friend I am helping will say something in passing that seems significant. I don't want to stop his train of thought, but I really want to follow up on this point, so I'll jot down a word or a phrase, just enough to jog my memory. Later in the conversation, or even the next time we are together, I'll say, "You mentioned. . . Can you tell me more about this?"

How Often to Meet

How often and for how long should you try to see someone? Much of that depends on the nature of the problem that has brought your friend to you for help. Problems that have been building up over a long time are not solved with a single cup of coffee or even several, so I often say, "You know, I really appreciate your sharing your heart with me today. I think I can help you work through this, but we need some time to talk, pray, and think. How about making a commitment to get together with me for the next six Wednesdays?" Or I might say, "How about having lunch with me every other week for the next couple of months? As I get to know you better, I can better answer your questions about. . ."

Eventually, you will sense that you have taken the person as far as you think you can take her. You may feel rather pleased that things have gone well and that the issue that first prompted the question, "What do you think I should do?" has been resolved. At that point you may want to say, "I think you are pretty well on top of the situation. I want you to know that if you need help, I'm available, but I don't think we need to get together as regularly. Let's set a date for lunch or coffee in two months and talk things over then."

What Can Your Friend Expect from You?

The first time I sit down with someone, I realize that the primary purpose of our time together is to work through a problem, so I strive to put the person at ease by telling him or her three things. You will want to take these three statements and personalize them so you are comfortable saying them, but in your own words you need to convey the following ideas.

I often tell people, "I wish I had the ability to look into your heart and say, 'Ah, I see clearly what you need!' I'd write a prescription and send you to the druggist with the assurance that if you take three little white pills in the morning and two blue-and-green ones in the evening, the problem will go away in four to seven days."

Then I remind them, "You've got to remember that the intangible problems of the heart are far more difficult than physical problems." I sometimes point out a little scar on my collarbone and tell the person that one day I was showering and felt a little lump. When Dr. Chase saw it, he said, "That's got to come out right now!" It did! A few minutes later I left his office minus the lump, with a Band-Aid marking the spot where the problem had been. But problems of the heart can't be surgically removed, X-rayed, or submitted to CAT scans for immediate evaluation.

Difficulties that have been in the making for months, or even years, will not disappear in a matter of weeks. But while you need to remind your friend of this fact, at the same time you should assure her that there is a way out, and whether or not you see it at the moment, you will stay with her until a solution is found. The fact that you have hope gives confidence to a person who may have given up.

I Will Keep Your Confidence: You Can Trust Me

The person who comes to you is pretty sure that you are trustworthy, but when you say these words out loud, you help your friend risk being vulnerable enough to tell you exactly what is happening in her life. Sometimes I say, "When you go to your family doctor, you trust him to keep your confidence, and what you're sharing with me now is a lot more important than a lump here or there."

Sometimes you will find yourself counseling people in your church, your Bible study, your company, or your neighborhood, people with whom you have social contact. Obviously, then, the relationship you have with the person you are trying to help is going to be different from a doctor-patient relationship. The doctor, whom you usually see garbed in green in the presence of his nurse, seldom bumps into you on the street or at a social event.

Don't you feel funny knowing certain intimate things about people with whom you have social contact? you may be thinking. No, not at all. Some of my best friends (actually, many of them) are people whom I first got to know in a counseling situation because of deep personal problems that, in time, were successfully resolved. Today I watch their children growing up, and I thank God I had the privilege of helping them make decisions that kept their homes together. The conversations that took place and the situations my friends confronted are a sealed chapter, covered with God's forgiveness and the forgetfulness of real love and friendship.

Let me give you a word of warning, though: Resist the temptation to mention a person's problem for prayer in your prayer group or Bible study. "But," you may say, "the Bible says we need to pray for each other." Right; I agree. You *should* pray. During your personal prayer time, carry your friend's needs to the Lord. Offer to pray regularly with him. But don't you dare break his confidence under the thinly veiled guise of asking others for prayer. When my daughter read this section, she penciled a note of sarcasm in the margin of the manuscript: "Christians don't gossip; they just share prayer requests."

Keep the confidences of people who trust you enough to open their hearts to you. Your failure to do this is not only poor judgment but will ruin your friendship. It destroys your effectiveness as a coffee cup counselor, and it may diminish the possibility of your friends' resolving their problems.

I Cannot Help You Unless
I Know Where You Hurt

But after I say this, I want to make sure that the person to whom I'm talking doesn't think I'm saying, "Let's hurry up and get on with this; you're wasting my time," so I add, "We've got plenty of time. I know that it may not be easy for you to talk about some things, so why don't you start at the beginning and tell me what brought you here for help?"

Some people, however, really don't want help when they ask, "What do you think I should do?" They may be seeking your opinion like a politician asking advice from his constituency. What you think or say doesn't really matter, because they have already decided on a course of action. They simply want to add your name to the roster of people who have endorsed their decision, provided you agree.

I have talked with people who had gone to at least a half dozen other people before me. "Why did you come to me?" I ask, and I usually hear something like, "Well, I didn't like what so-and-so told me."

There's one more issue you will eventually face. When you succeed in helping someone, on occasion, the person you are helping begins to lean on you and becomes emotionally dependent. You begin to feel smothered, and you realize it isn't good for the person you are helping, either. Symptoms of this are daily phone calls, consultations before even the smallest dcisions are made, and the constant request for your nod of approval.

What do you do when a person calls you every day and talks for an hour over the phone, giving you a word-by-word account of "He said. . ." and "I said. . ." and "He said. . ."?

Suggestion: Say, "This is so important that we should talk about this in person. Let's not mull this over on the phone. Come over to my house Friday morning at ten. We'll have a cup of coffee and you can tell me all about it." Your friend, though, may be the mother of five, as well as working part-time in the school cafeteria. She can't be at your house Friday at ten.

In such a case, outline a program of positive action, some kind of homework that relates to the problem: a book or article that speaks to your friend's need, a pertinent verse of Scripture that you ask her to memorize, a tape that you want her to hear.

Then when your friend calls the next time, say, "Before we get into this today, I'd like to ask, have you read the book [or memorized the verse or listened to the tape] I gave you?" When the answer is, "No," and you sense that the person wants only sympathy and not help, say, "I can't really be effective in helping you until you read [or memorize or listen to] it. When you do, call me back and we'll get together."

When a child learns to walk, a parent offers support and help—but gradually, as the child becomes stronger, the parent doesn't have to provide the same help. That is the way it must be with those we counsel. If you understand the real goals of counseling, you will be able to help the person you are counseling move toward psychological independence.

We'll discuss this process in the next chapter.

QUESTIONS FOR THOUGHT AND DISCUSSION

1. The Bible suggests that we should be willing to give of ourselves without reserve, just as Christ did. Why, then, do you think Dr. Sala recommends that you not always "drop everything" when someone asks you for help?

2. In your own words, rephrase the three statements Dr. Sala says we should convey to people we are counseling.

3. Why do you think each of these statements is important to the counseling process?

4. Dr. Sala suggests a couple of ways to handle a friend who has become too dependent on your support. Can you think of any others?

Chapter 4

The Counseling Process

When you set out on a journey by automobile and you are unsure of your way, you take a road map, something that can guide you toward your destination. In a very real sense, God has also given us a road map for our lives: the Bible. His Word gives us some idea of where we should be headed.

When a person has gotten off the right road, if you know the geography, you say to him, "You can't get where you want to go from here. You need to go back and take another road." By the same token, when you are familiar with Scripture and you can look at a friend's problem objectively, you will have some idea what she needs to do to get back on the right track.

Three objectives serve as goals, and though progress never takes a straight line, you move toward these objectives as you would geographic landmarks in the distance. You can observe progress as you pass through these three phases in the helping process. The following outline may help you see what I'll be discussing in the rest of the chapter.

The Three Goals of Counseling

1) Identify the problem.
2) Analyze the options and the consequences

of accepting or rejecting each one.
3) Help your friend discover and choose the will of God.

The counseling process is like a time line along which a person must move before a problem can be effectively resolved.

The Counseling Process

PHASE 1: EXPLORATION
Goal: Identify the problem.
What the Counselor Does: Listens,
evaluates, questions, ponders, clarifies.

PHASE 2: ENCOUNTER
Goal: Analyze the available options.
What the Counselor Does:
Helps the counselee confront the consequences of each option.

PHASE 3: RECONSTRUCTION
Goal: Discover and choose God's will.
What the Counselor Does:
Motivates; guides through repentance and reconstruction.

As you work through a given problem with someone, you will find that these three phases of the counseling process are not marked by specific boundaries, any more than the passing from youth to adulthood to middle age has signposts along the way. But like maturation, the counseling process involves definite transitions that are necessary to resolve the problem.

Phase 1: Exploration

During this period you listen, evaluate, question, and ponder. Like a physician who examines a patient for the first time, you are trying to get the picture clearly. You understand that initially the person who comes to you for help is deciding if you can be trusted. At the same time, her emotions and feelings may be confused. Life doesn't come to us in neat little packages, and you may get the story in bits and pieces.

This first phase of counseling may take an hour or two, or several weeks. After all, you may be the first person with whom your friend has ever talked about her problem, and as you listen, you may only gradually begin to see the picture develop. You have to see the problem clearly before you can help your friend look for solutions. This first phase of counseling relates very closely to goal 1—identifying the problem. This is such a critical part of the counseling process that we will talk about how to accomplish this both in this chapter and then again in the one to follow.

Phase 2: Encounter

Once the problem is clearly identified in your mind, you want to help your friend see the options and the consequences of accepting or rejecting each one. In the first phase of the counseling process, you ask questions to help you get the picture. In the second phase, you continue asking questions, but for an entirely different reason: You want the counselee to face the consequences of each possible option.

This is when you will need to say something like: "If you do this, what are the consequences of that decision? Are you willing to live with those consequences?" During this crucial period of time, you have to accept the risk that your relationship with your friend-counselee may become strained. After all, your friend will probably associate you with the consequence which he or she dislikes facing. You face the risk of seeing the relationship with your friend strained; however, the risk has to be taken before you can move into the final phase that brings healing and resolution.

Phase 3: Reconstruction

At the beginning of this phase, the person you are helping makes a decision. From all the options you have discussed, he chooses one. He accepts the fact that God does have direction for him, and he believes that one particular path must be taken, regardless of how easy or difficult it may be. Here your big task is to provide loving support and help your friend follow through with the decision he has made. Finally, when he is strong enough and mature enough to handle the problem alone, you have worked yourself out of a job.

Now let's go deeper as we consider how to help the person who has turned to you for help.

THE FIRST GOAL OF COUNSELING: IDENTIFY THE PROBLEM

You may be thinking, *Isn't the problem really obvious?* But what may be totally obvious to you may not be obvious at all to the person whom you are trying to help. And what may be obvious to her may not be at all clear to her husband or boyfriend. Long ago, the wise man who penned Proverbs 16:2 recognized this as he wrote, "All the ways of a man are pure in his own eyes. . . ." The word translated "pure" in the New King James Version also means "upright" or "just."

Quite often we tend to magnify the faults of others and minimize our own; when a problem occurs, we see ourselves in a different light than others do. Actually, there are three perspectives that confront the person you are helping—how she sees herself, how her mate or the other involved person sees her, and how God sees her.

Believe me, my experience, gained through many years of counseling and working with people, has convinced me that these three seldom match up. But until the person who has come for help gains these three perspectives, she will not see the necessity of moving into the second phase of counseling. Let me illustrate.

Jack and Michelle have been married for eighteen years. He's forty and she is thirty-eight. When they got married, she weighed 103 pounds and had a perfect hourglass figure. Now, approaching their middle years, everything has changed. He's obviously out of shape, and Michelle has added more weight than she would care to admit.

When they were first married, they had a tough time financially. But during Michelle's difficult first pregnancy, they both became believers in Jesus Christ and joined a church. Michelle volunteered to help in the church nursery, taking her turn along with the other young mothers, and Jack often attended the men's fellowship, especially when his fishing buddy Pete offered to go with him.

To supplement their income, Michelle soon went to work. Because Jack was an electrical engineer, his income rose, but so did his responsibilities. When babies two and three came along, Michelle's income was an absolute necessity. Michelle's life was filled with activities—church, PTA, new computer programs at work. Meanwhile, when Jack was promoted to management, he began traveling at least one weekend out of four. With Jack away from home or else buried in his den catching up on paperwork, their marriage sank into the morass of middle-age boredom.

At first there wasn't anything really wrong; their relationship just seemed a little flatter, a little less exciting and interesting. When they were together, they either had nothing to say or else they picked at the little things they didn't like about each other.

Michelle thought about their relationship a lot, and she had so much she wanted to say about the two of them. She wanted to walk hand in hand together as they used to do at the beach. She yearned to have those quiet times they had when they were first married and had nothing but each other, when night after night they would sit on the old worn rug in front of the fireplace and pour out their hearts to each other. She wished she could say, "Jack, remember how you used to run your hands through my hair and tell me I was the most beautiful girl you ever saw? You never do that anymore." Lost in the passing of time was the intimacy that had meant so much—the complete honesty and openness they once had with each other. She remembered the time she was afraid to get a Novocain shot at the dentist, and instead of saying, "That's dumb! Nothing to be afraid of," Jack took off an hour early from work and went to the dentist with her. But all of that was history.

One day she interrupted the Dodgers' game as she blurted out, "Jack, if you weren't so addicted to that stupid TV, you might have time for me and your kids."

Adding insult to injury, Jack barely looked up from the game. "All right," he grunted, his eyes on the screen, "what do you want?"

She tried to communicate her feelings, but all she got back was a brilliant response like, "Yeah. Sure. Why not? I couldn't care less."

She felt rejected and hurt.

When Michelle later brought up the possibility of professional counseling, Jack was irate. "I don't need to talk to some shrink. Our marriage is as good as those airheads who think they know it all and charge eighty-five dollars an hour. And, besides, if we can't make it work, nobody can do it for us."

Within six months Michelle had gained another ten pounds. She joined a weight-loss group, but nothing really seemed to help. And then Julie was hired as Jack's new secretary.

A divorcee with two small children, Julie was trim and pretty, like Michelle had been in the early years of their marriage. Jack didn't say anything, but he noticed.

"You know my wife is always complaining. . . because, well, she says I'm a lousy communicator, and I suppose she is right," Jack said to Julie one day as he finished a dictation session.

"Nonsense," Julie replied. "I've found you to be interesting, informative, and. . .well, nice."

"Really?" Jack basked in the compliment.

That's how it started. But after that, Jack and Julie's conversations became longer and more intimate. Eventually Julie told Jack how her husband had walked out on her and left her for someone more exciting. Jack began to share how flat his marriage had become.

At first it was just talk, nothing more. But without realizing what he was doing, Jack began to think up excuses to spend more time with Julie—working on the end-of-the-year report at night together or having dinner planning the convention.

These innocent meetings all changed the night Julie dropped a piece of paper on the floor beside his desk. As she leaned over to pick it up, her long brown hair fell against his cheek. Without thinking, Jack pulled her face close to his and kissed her.

Instead of pulling away, Julie said, "You shouldn't have done that. But it sure felt good. It's been so long since someone did that to me." Only a few days later, at a convention in Chicago, they just happened to find themselves in side-by-side hotel rooms—but the maid had to change only one set of linens.

For six months, Michelle never suspected the fact that she was sharing her husband with someone else. When Jack joined a gym and lost fifteen pounds, she just assumed he had started out on a new health kick. He still went to church occasionally, and he seemed more engrossed in his work than ever before.

When Michelle finally learned about Jack's affair, she was both crushed and furious. There were tears and harsh, angry words—plenty of them. Both accused each other of being the real problem.

"Let's talk to Pastor Tom at church!" Michelle pled.

"No way! We're not washing our dirty linen in front of other people."

Jack was torn. At times he didn't know his own feelings. Sometimes he regretted what he was doing, especially when he picked up his three year old in his arms. He remembered how he and Michelle had prayed so hard together when she was six months pregnant and it looked like she was going to lose the baby.

Lying in bed at night, hearing Michelle sob in her sleep, he knew how much he was hurting her. He wouldn't admit it, but in the quiet of the night he knew God was saying, *Hey, this is not what you really want, nor what I want. What you are doing is wrong. You've come too far, and I've helped you too much already for you to blow it now. Straighten out your life. Get help!*

Jack's work was affected, too. He couldn't concentrate. The picture of Michelle and the kids was still on the desk; but Julie was just outside his office door at her desk. . .and available.

The next weekend was the opening of the fishing season, a ritual he and his old fishing buddy Pete had observed since they were kids. No way was he going to miss this one. So the evening of opening day, when he and Pete were at the fishing lodge in Wisconsin, they sat in front of the old stone fireplace and began to talk. After swapping yarns about the "big ones" they used to catch, Pete finally said, "Hey, Jack, got something on your mind? You've been as uptight as a cat in a room full of rocking chairs."

Everything came out that night, every bit of it,

how the marriage had grown stale, how Michelle had gotten overweight, how all she did was complain, and how beautiful and available Julie was. At two o'clock in the morning, the question finally came, "Pete, you seem to have your head screwed on pretty straight. What do you think I should do?"

Jack would never, ever have gone to a professional for counseling. But with a friend with whom he felt comfortable, he opened his heart and sincerely reached for help. What a tremendous opportunity for Pete, the fishing buddy who took Jack to the men's fellowship at church!

Now as a friend and a counselor, Pete's first task is to help Jack see himself as he really is. To do this, Pete will need to help Jack see himself from Michelle's viewpoint (and possibly the perspective of his kids, ages three to eight, as well). Last and most importantly, Pete needs to help Jack see himself as God sees him.

How Is This Accomplished?

Through penetrating questions! If Pete is to be effective as a counselor-friend, he has to help Jack see the full picture.

It isn't difficult for Pete to get the picture of how Jack views himself. Jack sees himself as a red-blooded male with sexual needs that are not properly being met in his marriage. He tells Pete how repulsive it has become to make love with a woman who is sixty pounds overweight and constantly nags at him. He also believes that what he is doing isn't so bad. "After all," he reminds Pete, "everybody is doing it these days, even preachers." He justifies himself further as he launches into a tirade against a local pastor who ran off with the church organist. He sees nothing wrong in spending time and money on Julie. "I haven't hurt my kids or Michelle," he tells Pete.

How does Michelle see him? This is a little harder for Jack to face. She sees him as a traitor to his vows, as an adulterer who cheated on her, and as a thief who has taken money and gifts that should have been hers and their children's, and given them to his secretary. Once Pete can get Jack to face this perspective on his behavior, Jack may begin to feel a little guilt.

That will get Jack ready for Pete's last question: How does God view what has taken place? When I am working through a situation like this with someone, I often ask, "How do you think God feels about what has happened?" At first, the answers I hear are usually trite, like, "Oh, I think He understands; after all, He made me the way I am." Or "I don't know; never thought much about it." At this point I say, "Let's take a look at what God says about our lives in His Book, the Bible."

I should point out here that what the Bible says is sometimes in conflict with some theories that are embraced by secular counseling disciplines. Let's make sure we understand what God does say about personal responsibility.

The Bible stresses the individual's responsibility. From the very beginning of time, human beings have sought to blame their failures either on someone else or on circumstances over which they had no control. Remember that Adam evaded responsibility for taking the fruit by blaming Eve: "The woman whom You gave to be with me, she gave me of the tree, and I ate" (Genesis 3:12). Adam was saying, "Look, God, it's partly Your fault because You put her here in the garden with me, and she took the fruit. All I did was innocently eat it." His reply to God's question about eating the fruit was a far cry from the truth: "Yes, I took the fruit of my own volition, and I am completely responsible for my actions!"

A passage I almost always use to establish personal responsibility is Ezekiel 18:20–23, which reads:

> *"The soul who sins shall die. The son shall not bear the guilt of the father, nor the father bear the guilt of the son. The righteousness of the righteous shall be upon himself, and the wickedness of the wicked shall be upon himself.*
>
> *"But if a wicked man turns from all his sins which he has committed, keeps all My statutes, and does what is lawful and right, he shall surely live; he shall not die.*
>
> *"None of the transgressions which he has committed shall be remembered against him. . . .*

*"Do I have any pleasure at all that the
wicked should die?" says the Lord GOD,
"and not that he should turn from his ways
and live?"*

When it comes to infidelity in marriage, several Scripture passages speak clearly. You need to know where these are and be able to turn to them. Note the following passages: "It is God's will that you should be sanctified: that you should avoid sexual immorality; that each of you should learn to control his own body in a way that is holy and honorable, not in passionate lust like the heathen. . ." (1 Thessalonians 4:3–5 NIV).

Jesus denounced adultery, as recorded in Matthew 5:27–30 and 19:3–10, emphatically saying that if a man even lusted after a woman, he had committed adultery with her in his heart. (See also Mark 10:1–12 and Luke 16:18 for parallel renderings.)

People often blame their physical chemistry, as Jack did: "I can't help doing what I do because God made me the way I am!" Or they blame circumstances or society. They explain away their conduct by excusing themselves because of social pressures.

But God says you are responsible for what you do! Another passage that is often helpful to establish moral responsibility is the story of David and Bathsheba. When God sent the prophet Nathan to David to confront him with the enormity of his sin, Nathan told a story about two men, a rich man who had flocks and herds, and a poor man who had only one little ewe lamb. A traveler came to visit, and instead of using one of his own many sheep for a meal for the visitor, the rich man killed the poor man's one lamb. When David heard the story, he burned with anger and vowed that the man who did this must surely die. "Then Nathan said to David, 'You are the man!' " (2 Samuel 12:7).

Notice that Nathan did not begin by confronting David with his guilt; instead, he led David to the point where he was the one to make the accusations. One way you can achieve the same goal is by asking questions to establish responsibility rather than by making statements. Yes, you can tell someone how wrong they are or what a stupid thing they have done, and you may be able to generate a considerable amount of guilt (or anger). But your goal is not to make the person defensive; what you want to do instead is help her accept the full responsibility for her actions.

When David finally accepted his full guilt, it hit him with a tremendous impact. "I have sinned against the LORD," he cried (2 Samuel 12:13). His repentance and deep sorrow for what he had done were sincere. David tells of his remorse and anguish in Psalm 51: "I acknowledge my transgressions, and my sin is always before me. Against You, You only, have I sinned, and done this evil in Your sight. . ." (verses 3–4).

At this point, David saw himself as God saw him,

as he really was, and as others saw him. Only then was he prepared to face the implications of what he had done and experience the reconstruction process that followed.

If Pete wants to help Jack see himself from God's perspective, Pete will eventually need to focus on how God looks at the situation. Pete could say something like, "You know, Jack, I remember a situation in the Bible where someone worked himself into a corner, kind of like you've done. Let's take a look at it together," and then go to the passage about David. Next, Pete can ask penetrating questions such as these: "As terrible as David's sin may appear, do you think God views what you have done any differently? How does God view what's taken place?"

Identifying the Problem Leads to Accepting the Responsibility

Dr. Frank Pittman is a psychiatrist who specializes in why people become involved in relationships outside of marriage. In his book *Private Lies: Infidelity and the Betrayal of Intimacy*, Pittman tells of interviewing one hundred couples who describe in detail why they got involved with someone else. "It was not sex but a lack of intimacy that had compelled them to have an affair," says Pittmann.[1]

What Jack and Michelle once had, what she desperately wanted again, was intimacy—commitment, mutual trust, openness, total honesty, and the sort of vulnerability where both were absolutely transparent with each other. Jack's lack of communication made him distant and less intimate.

Marriage is a husband and wife's commitment to try to meet each other's needs, and those needs go far beyond sexual needs. While most men think only in terms of environmental needs (food, shelter, and clothing), a woman's needs are far more complex. Jack had never considered the fact that Michelle's needs included communication, intimacy, and a feeling of self-worth. His comments about her weight did nothing to improve her self-image. (In fact, her trips to the refrigerator had become a reaction against his lack of communication, which became a vicious circle: The more she ate, the more weight she gained; and the more weight she gained, the less attention Jack wanted to give her; and so she ate more. . . .) Remember, when they were first married, he had often told her how beautiful she was. Michelle missed those days.

A man who accepts responsibility for his family must also make provisions for the needs of his wife, just as she must meet those same needs in her husband. Paul had strong words for husbands who give little thought to the needs of their wives: "If anyone does not provide for his own. . .he has denied the faith and is worse than an unbeliever" (1 Timothy 5:8). When our needs are not met, our sexual lives are the first area to be negatively affected—and when a reluctant or insecure partner does not meet the sexual needs of a mate, a vacuum is created that another person may satisfy.

When I sense that this situation may exist, I ask, "Could you have been partly responsible for your mate's actions by your indifference? By failing to meet his sexual needs? By a lack of interest in his world?" Or, "Have you attempted to view this situation from your wife's perspective? Tell me honestly —what would you possibly have done if you had been in her shoes?"

Meeting each other's needs is vital. A few years ago, a young man named William Glasser was in medical school preparing to become a psychiatrist. He began to reject many of the premises of modern psychiatry, especially Sigmund Freud's theory of psychoanalysis. By the time Glasser finished his evolution of thought, he had pioneered a new approach to meeting the needs of people, which he called "reality therapy" (his book bears this title).[2] Apart from organic illnesses, such as schizophrenia, Glasser says that there is no such thing as mental illness. He contends that mental illnesses such as neuroses and psychoses are but masks or symptoms of irresponsibility.

Glasser believes that every person—whether a gray-haired grandmother or a tiny baby—has two basic needs: the need to love and be loved, and the need to feel worthwhile to one's self and to other people. When these needs are met, Glasser believes, people act in a responsible fashion. When these needs are not met, irresponsibility, often labeled as mental illness, results.

Glasser, a Roman Catholic by faith, doesn't attempt to correlate what he believes with what the Bible teaches, yet those two needs—love and fulfillment—are definitely within the broad framework of what the Bible says about our lives. The Bible, however, goes beyond these in asserting that every person has a third need—the need for security that is met by a vertical relationship with God.

Glasser would advise Julie against a relationship with Jack—not because God views it as sin, but because her needs cannot be met by a casual affair. Along with Glasser, many other psychiatrists today are also saying what the Word of God has been saying for centuries: "You are responsible, and you can change" (though most of them do not accept the biblical concepts of sin and redemption).

One of the newest voices is the British psychiatrist Garth Wood, who contends that neurosis is a myth. He says "moral therapy" is the cure for people who have violated their own ethics, meaning you stop blaming the environment or illness or other people and begin reflecting on your inner values (whatever they may be). Wrongdoing, in Wood's view, is not the violation of God's laws, but rather the violation of your moral system, which effectively eliminates any objective criteria of morality or right or wrong. Wood's approach is pragmatic—if it gives relief, it must be right.

Of course, I don't agree with that premise; the Bible lays down very clear moral guidelines, and God has commanded us to serve others, not ourselves.

THE SECOND GOAL OF COUNSELING: ANALYZE THE AVAILABLE OPTIONS AND THE CONSEQUENCES OF ACCEPTING OR REJECTING EACH ONE

During the first phase of counseling, you are trying to get the picture, but merely seeing the picture clearly doesn't change anything, which means you have to move into the second phase: encounter. Here you want to explore the courses of action. You must confront your friend with the consequences of his action, as hard as it may be to face them. At this point, the past ceases to be important. The future is everything, and the present decides what the future will be.

Don't let this one slide or pass over it casually. This phase is important. If we default on it, the consequences of our actions will overtake us. We then bear the natural consequences, which in Jack's case would probably be a divorce. When we refuse to recognize the consequences of our actions, we must live with the results of poor choices.

The big question with which you must confront your friend is this: "Where do we go from here? What plan do you have?" The question is usually greeted with a response of, "I don't know!" So then I ask, "What options do you see? Let's start making a list of the options, and then, once we have the list, let's consider what would happen with each choice."

In Jack's situation, he has three choices:

- He can do nothing at all and continue his relationship with Julie
- He can lie to Michelle and continue to see Julie on the side
- He can break off the relationship with Julie, which probably means finding a new secretary as well

You could come up with the options yourself (they may be clear to you), but don't do it. You want your friend to face these options. Even more importantly, you want your friend to recognize what is going to happen as the result of the choice which is made.

Once Jack listed his options, I would move on to the next question: What are the consequences of each?

Choosing to do nothing at all is the choice to continue to see bitterness and resentment destroy his relationship with Michelle. At times I remind people that they may start over, but they never start again. I remind them of their first kiss, the purity of their love, the first child, and the joy they experienced sharing what little they had together. These experiences can never be repeated with another person.

A powerful consideration Jack needs to face is the impact of his affair on his children. Dr. Paul Popenoe, a longtime authority on the American family, contends that when a couple with two children divorce, the lives of at least twelve people are affected: the couple who agree to disagree, the parents of each spouse, the two children who grow up with inadequate financial and emotional support, and even their children when they marry. What happens between two people in marriage vitally affects the future of everyone in the family circle.

If Jack chooses to ignore this issue, he is making a decision to see his family disintegrate further. Prodding deeper, I'd ask, "Is this situation good?" Then I would turn to James 4:17 and ask Jack to read it aloud. It says, "To him who knows to do good and does not do it, to him it is sin."

If the point hasn't already been clearly established, right here is a good point to label this situation for what it is in the sight of God: sin! If Jack recognizes his sinfulness, then the door opens for forgiveness and healing.

He can choose to lie to Michelle and continue to see Julie on the side. But trying to put a distance between the two women inevitably compounds the problem. Proverbs 28:13 says, "He who covers his sins will not prosper, but whosoever confesses and forsakes them will have mercy." If Jack succeeds in fooling Michelle (and on occasion you will talk with someone whose husband or wife isn't aware of what is going on), Jack faces the consequences of living a life of deception, covering his tracks while he postpones the eventual consequences of discovery.

In this case, his situation is much like the youth who had borrowed his father's car without permission. As he was returning from his joyride, he failed to see a car coming from a side street and ran into the other car, damaging the front of his father's car. As he stood beside the crumpled fender, he closed his eyes and said, "Dear God, I pray this didn't happen!"

There is no way you can unscramble scrambled eggs. Certain actions will carry inevitable consequences, some of which are painful. Leaving one woman for another does not eliminate the responsibility a man has to his children, regardless of the failure of the other parent. Jack fathered those children, and he bears a responsibility for them.

That leaves us with Jack's last option: He can break off the relationship with Julie and go to work on his relationship with Michelle. This takes us to the final goal of counseling.

THE THIRD GOAL OF COUNSELING: HELP THE COUNSELEE TO DISCOVER AND CHOOSE THE WILL OF GOD FOR HIS LIFE

In the second phase of the counseling process, the issue of wrongdoing must be faced. Glossing over sin or excusing it on the basis of human weakness offers no hope for removing it and overcoming it. But acknowledging it—calling it what it really is—opens up the path of restoration, which is the third phase of the counseling process.

As you analyze the consequences of the options, you then have to bring the one you are helping to a place of confrontation with the will of God. Obviously, it cannot be the will of God for a person to continue in any sinful relationship or situation.

The concept behind the Greek word *harmatia,* usually translated "sin" in the New Testament, is that of missing the mark, of falling short of the target. Acts of wrongdoing have taken your friend outside of God's will; they have fallen short of the mark which God wanted attained. To right the wrong requires positive action, which means breaking habit patterns that have become pleasant and perhaps enjoyable.

At this point, the relationship you have with your friend is tremendously important. Sometimes simply being there—encouraging, loving, and reinforcing without condemnation—is the additional strength that your friend needs to do the right thing, especially when he or she knows what is right but lacks the courage to take the necessary steps. Many Christians whose marriages fail fall into this category, and the input of a friend who cares enough to hold someone accountable could have made the difference in helping to save a troubled marriage.

What Is Necessary to Bring Healing to a Broken Relationship?

The process of reconciliation can be thus illustrated:

OFFENDING PERSON		OFFENDED PERSON
Confession	⟷	Forgiveness
Repentance	⟷	Restoration

In an old fishing lodge, as the sun was coming up over the horizon, Pete and Jack knelt and prayed together. Jack wept tears of repentance. He freely confessed that he didn't know how his marriage with Michelle would come together, but he knew that he had to ask Michelle's forgiveness and ask her to try one more time. Instead of going fishing, the two men drove home, and a tearful reunion with Michelle followed.

How much should someone like Jack tell the one who has been offended and hurt? Confession to God and the one who has been hurt is necessary—but a recital or catalog of transgressions is not. I do not believe that every morbid detail has to be reviewed in the presence of a mate. God knows already, and the husband or wife knows that he or she has been betrayed. The details will only hurt them even more.

Jack needs to know that God will forgive him and remove his sin. (See passages like Psalm 51; Isaiah 43:25; Psalm 103:12; 1 John 1:9.) Then once the sin has been confessed, the offending spouse needs to ask forgiveness of the one he or she has hurt. What a joy to pray with someone who confesses his wrong-doing before the Father and then does the same before his mate!

But for healing to take place, the one who has been hurt must extend complete forgiveness. The offending person cannot merely say, "I have done [whatever] and I am sorry that I have hurt you." He or she must also ask, "Will you forgive me for what I have done to you?" The transaction is not complete until the one who has been hurt says, "Yes, I will forgive you!"

A couple came to me for counseling with a serious problem—very serious. The husband was trying to remodel the kitchen, and his wife didn't much care for the plans. The husband was under stress at work and at the same time he felt he was bending over backward to do the work on the kitchen in the first place, so he became angry with his wife's objections. He forgot that she was the one who would spend many hours in the remodeled kitchen. Frustrated and furious, he had doubled up his fist and let her have it. (Though I can understand the anger, I can never justify physical violence in marriage.)

"Has this happened before?" I asked the husband. He hesitated a bit and then told me this was the first time. But when I asked the wife the same question separately, she said it had happened before, but she couldn't remember how many times.

"Have you ever forgiven him?" I asked.

"Not really! I'm finished. I just can't take this any longer," she replied.

I began working first with him, then with both of them. Eventually, he came to understand that stress must be handled without allowing his anger to spill over on her or the children. With tears in his eyes, he asked, "Honey, will you forgive me?"

She hesitated and then quietly responded, "Yes, I forgive you!"

Later that wife told me, "You know, something changed inside when I said, 'Yes, I'll forgive you.' I had never really forgiven him before, even though he'd said he was sorry. This time it was different!"

I repeat: The offending person must ask for forgiveness—and just as important, the offended person must extend forgiveness. Repentance must be met with reconciliation—or restoration. No matter how repentant the offending person may be, if the offended party will not really extend restoration to that person, genuine healing cannot take place; the wound continues to fester, and it will eventually destroy a relationship.

The offended person can all too easily continue to remind her mate of the wrongdoing. Yes, I understand that once the wall of trust has been broken down, rebuilding it is a long and even painful process. But it must be undertaken.

For a long time after the relationship with Julie ended, whenever Jack was late coming home, or had to be out of town, or received a phone call from an unidentified person of the opposite sex, the memories of his affair with Julie replayed in Michelle's mind. Jack understood that, and he did his best to let her know when he expected to be late and why. Meanwhile, Michelle had to remind herself that forgiveness isn't complete when we hold on to bitter memories and let them erode our peace of mind.

Shortly after his eventful fishing trip with Pete, Jack encouraged Julie to find work elsewhere, and Michelle took that as a real sign of his commitment to their marriage. Though some of Michelle's friends told her she was a fool to stay with Jack—and at times she really questioned whether it was the right thing to do—in her heart she realized she had much to gain by striving to forgive and rebuild.

Writing to the Ephesians about the importance of forgiveness, Paul said that God's forgiveness of us is the pattern we must follow as we forgive each other. "Be kind to one another, tenderhearted, forgiving one another, even as God in Christ forgave you" (Ephesians 4:32). Jesus said, "For if you forgive men when they sin against you, your heavenly Father will also forgive you. But if you do not forgive men their sins, your Father will not forgive your sins" (Matthew 6:14–15 NIV).

Why does God demand so forcefully that we forgive each other? Surely the answer must be the high cost that He paid to forgive us, giving His Son to be crucified at Calvary. He wants us to understand that forgiveness is truly a matter of life and death.

Maintaining a "holier than thou" attitude destroys the restoration process and often results in further infidelity. Let me give you an example.

The day after I spoke at a certain Bible school, a tearful young woman telephoned me. "I heard you speak yesterday," she began, "and I desperately need your help." She said her husband was preparing for the ministry, while at the same time he was making her life miserable. She said, "When I was a teenager, I had sex with my boyfriend. But then I found the Lord as my Savior and realized that what we were doing was wrong, and I broke it off. Then just before I married, I felt that I had to tell my fiancé that I was not a virgin and confess what had happened." Sobbing, she added, "But now that we're married, he wants more details, and I've told him everything there is to tell. He yells at me, 'You are no good; you aren't worthy of me; you are nothing but a slut!' "

"Would you have your husband call me tomorrow?" I asked.

The next day the young man called me. I began to talk about forgiveness, about accepting each other because God has forgiven us, but I got nowhere. Finally I said, "Suppose that I had a machine that could read your thoughts, and I brought it to your church on Sunday and flashed every thought you have had this past week on a screen for everyone to see. Would you be embarrassed?"

I had him and he knew it! He admitted that he would feel truly embarrassed.

Then I shared the words of Jesus: "You have heard that it was said to those of old, "You shall not commit adultery." But I say to you that whoever looks at a woman to lust for her has already committed adultery with her in his heart" (Matthew 5:27–28).

"You not only would be ashamed, you would crawl under the nearest chair and hide your face in shame, right?"

He admitted it!

Forgiveness that says, "Okay, I'll forgive you this time, but if you ever do it again, we're through!" isn't forgiveness. It is merely probation, and probation is not the same as restoration.

Forgiveness involves God, the offended, and the offending. All three must come together for real healing to take place.

In Jack and Michelle's case, real forgiveness and healing took between six months and a year. Pete was a tremendous help to both Jack and Michelle during this time. Pete was enough older than Jack to counsel him as a "father figure," and he and Jack began meeting weekly to work though the process of healing the broken relationship. Jack agreed to be accountable to Pete, confronting the issues and slowly reconstructing his marriage.

What happened to Jack and Michelle was painful, and rebuilding the relationship didn't come easily —but it did come. Looking back on the process, both Jack and Michelle would tell you it was the best decision they ever made.

Before we begin a new chapter, I'd like to close on a positive note. As Frank Pittman has observed, "Infidelity is the primary disrupter of families, the most dreaded and devastating experience in a marriage, and the most universally accepted justification for divorce"[3] —but unfaithfulness doesn't have to end in divorce. When people forgive each other, seek God's healing power, and rebuild the bridges of communication, a broken marriage can be helped. It happened to Jack and Michelle.

QUESTIONS FOR
THOUGHT AND DISCUSSION

1. In a counseling situation, why is it important to identify the problem before you do anything else?

2. List other Bible characters, who, like David, sinned and had to confess their failure before they could go on to be used by God.

3. Why must the person recognize for herself her options and their consequences? Why can't we simply save time and point these out to the people we are counseling?

4. Why do you think it is so important for the offended person to extend forgiveness?

CHAPTER 5

DIAGNOSE THE PROBLEM BUT TREAT THE WHOLE PERSON

A little bit of knowledge is a dangerous thing! When I first began dispensing advice (may God forgive me!) I thought I had answers for most of life's problems, but looking back from the perspective of several decades of experience, I'm not sure now that I even understood the questions. Life is complex, and many of the problems that confront us defy simplistic, "Here's what to do in three easy steps" solutions.

Perhaps the greatest danger confronting those of you who want to help people is that you leap to conclusions as to what people's problems are before you have given them an adequate chance to get to the bottom of their troubles. We want to impress others with our wisdom—but in doing so, we risk making some foolish mistakes.

I am reminded of the young man who finished his degree in psychology and opened his office. Having put up the sign out front, he was waiting for the world to beat a path to his door. On the third day he heard the sound of footsteps coming down the hall. Intent on impressing his first client with his wisdom, he picked up the phone and said, "Yes, umm-huh!

I'm sure I can handle that problem. Yes, indeed. I see patients with that difficulty almost every day. Right! Friday at four. First office down the hall on the right! See you then."

Putting the phone down, he looked up at the young man standing in front of him and asked, "What can I do for you?"

"I've come to hook up your phone!" replied the visitor.

In the first phase of counseling, the exploratory phase, you, as counselor-friend, are trying to get a handle on what the issue really is. Our tendency is to isolate the spiritual problem—whatever it may be— and nail it to the floor with a Bible verse or two. *There*, we think smugly to ourselves, mentally dusting our hands, *I guess I took care of that problem.* Our task would be much easier if we could really deduce that all the problems requiring counseling were spiritual in nature and find Bible verses to neutralize the acid of discontent. Actually, however, most people's problems are a combination of the emotional, the physical, and the spiritual.

We tend to put life's difficulties in neat little boxes that we label as "emotional problems," "physical problems," or "spiritual problems." One of the first things you must learn, however, is that when some- one suffers, though the primary cause may be more directly related to a particular one of these three areas, all three areas are going to be affected.

When the level begins to drain in the honey- comb of life, it sinks in all three areas. I often use the illustration of a cylinder divided in three sections by a wire mesh; the liquids that fill it cannot be kept isolated from each other.

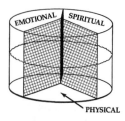

One of my complaints with secular psychiatry is that it fails to recognize humanity's spiritual nature. Genesis 2:7 says, "And the LORD God formed man of the dust of the ground, and breathed into his nostrils the breath of life; and man became a living being." Made in the image of God, human beings—even fallen human beings—have sensitivities and insights that none of God's other remarkable creatures possess.

Psychiatrists who practice their faith, of course, are in a much different position. They recognize that humans are a complex composite of the emotional, the physical, and the spiritual.

How Does Psychiatry Treat the Problems of People?

Secular psychiatry fails to see people as whole beings who are made up of emotions, body, and a spirit.

Instead, psychiatry tends to treat one aspect of a person, or maybe two, but it fails to meet the needs of the whole person. Today psychiatry practices one or more of the following basic forms of treatment:

Shock Therapy

Widely used a few years ago, this form of treatment is no longer (thank God!) used so extensively. Its success has been widely disputed, and the risk of potential damage to the brain is considerable.

Chemical Therapy

The slogan here is "better living through chemistry." Pharmaceuticals have become a major industry, with vast sums of money being spent for tranquilizers and a rainbow of drugs to elevate moods, suppress troubled feelings, or regulate emotions.

I recognize how important and helpful these drugs, on occasion, may be. Some people who suffer depression, for example, can find great relief with small doses of medication, which appears to balance a chemical deficiency in their body, just as glasses correct astigmatism of the eyeball. My objection, however, is to doctors who sedate and tranquilize all forms of problems instead of going to the bottom of the conflict.

Verbal Therapy

Often called "talking cures," this includes psycho-therapy. Through verbally analyzing a person's prob-lems, the person is expected to gain healing. In a sense those who practice what I call "bibliotherapy" (applying the principles of Scripture to the needs of men and women) are practicing verbal therapy.

Surgery

In severe cases of mental illness, neurosurgery is a last resort. Obviously, this treatment assumes that the person's problem is purely physical.

DIAGNOSING THE PHYSICAL

A wise counselor works in cooperation with medical science. Take, for example, Dr. Jack Morris, a Wash-ington, D.C. area pastor who is a trained psychother-apist. Morris works closely with a team of medical doctors who are dedicated Christians, and they all work in harmony with each other. At times Morris will refer a client to one of the physicians because he suspects that the client's emotional problem has physical roots. Likewise, when a person who comes for medical treatment is diagnosed as having a more emotional or spiritual problem, the physicians will send the person to Morris, who can help the patient work out the conflict. That makes sense!

How do you know when a problem may have physical roots? Much of the time you can quickly identify mood changes, depression, exhaustion, or boredom. In these cases, the person seems to be on good speaking terms with God. You can't really see a spiritual conflict; you can't see any root problems that would cause emotional problems. He is not in conflict with anybody. He seems to like his job. He doesn't feel trapped in a hopeless situation, such as working for someone he doesn't like and afraid of quitting, fearful of being unable to get another job. In this sort of case, you can legitimately suppose that a physical problem may produce these mood shifts.

"How long has it been since you have had a complete physical?" I often ask, and the usual reply is, "I don't remember, but a long time."

"Okay, before we get together again, I want you to go see your doctor, and I especially want him to check your blood sugar."

Why? Your diet and your blood sugar affect your emotions and your moods. For example, hypoglycemia, low blood sugar, may produce lethargy and even depression. Or a husband's inability to function sexually may not be emotional, but instead be the result of sugar diabetes that has been undiagnosed and untreated.

Telling people that God loves them and has a plan for their lives is good—but what they sometimes need is to realize that part of that plan is to let a doctor show them their physical problems and how to deal with them.

On one occasion, I counseled with a woman who told me how physically weary she was all the time, how she had to lie down periodically when she was doing her housework. She explained that sometimes she felt good, but at other times she really was hurting. She had gone to her doctor, who told her nothing was wrong with her and suggested she see a psychiatrist.

She wept bitter tears as she said, "Even my husband doesn't believe me when I tell him that I feel bad. He thinks that I'm faking it when I really hurt. Sometimes I think maybe I am going crazy!"

She wasn't crazy! She had lupus erythematosus (a blood disease), which was eventually diagnosed by a specialist. When she learned what her problem was, it didn't disappear, but the emotional conflict of thinking something was wrong with her mind was gone, and doctors began to treat the underlying source of her difficulty.

When you hurt physically, your spiritual life is also affected. The life of Elijah forcefully demonstrates that even spiritual giants get tired and discouraged and feel like quitting when they are exhausted physically. That's something we often forget.

The story of Elijah's confrontation with the 450 prophets of Baal is the stuff that missionaries like to put in their prayer letters. Tremendous victory! Fire from heaven falls and vindicates the lone prophet of

God. Even Lee Iacocca, who turned Chrysler around, couldn't brag about one like that. It was definitely a win-win situation.

But the next morning Jezebel, the wife of King Ahab, sent a messenger to Elijah, saying, "So let the gods do to me, and more also, if I do not make your life as the life of one of them by tomorrow about this time" (1 Kings 19:2). Suddenly, Elijah's sky turned gray, and the man of God turned and ran for his life. Is this the same spiritual giant who prayed down fire from heaven and single-handedly withstood the hundreds of false prophets? A giant—or a gnat who flees?

Same man, all right, but one who was physically and emotionally exhausted. "Elijah was a man just like us," says James (5:17 NIV), and in that statement is a tremendous insight. You aren't an iron man or an Amazonian woman! When you are physically exhausted, your emotional outlook and your relationship with God will be affected, which is why James instructed us to "pray for one another" (5:16). Elijah, along with scores of other biblical greats, had a physical body that could be weakened, and you must understand what's happening when you are affected the same way.

DIAGNOSING THE SPIRITUAL

I was a young pastor of my first church when Sam Jones met me in my office. This big bear of a man thrust a roll of bills into my hand as he said, "Here, this is the money for the shock treatments I was supposed to have but I no longer need!"

Sam had been in psychiatric treatment for several years without success. He would stay with one doctor for a while and when nothing happened, he would find another. The latest series of shock treatments hadn't helped him erase his memories of a troubled past. But when he received Jesus Christ as his Savior and came to understand that his past was forgiven, forgotten, and wiped away as though it had never taken place (see Psalm 103:12), his problem rapidly dissipated. Sam's psychiatrist recognized his improvement and canceled the shock treatments. This was one of my first encounters with the dynamic way in which Jesus Christ can totally change a person's emotional outlook.

No wonder, then, that Dr. Paul DuBois, a psychotherapist, says, "Religious faith is the best preventative against the maladies of the soul, mind, and body, and is the most powerful medicine we have ever discovered for curing them." I agree!

Over the years I have seen scores of men and women with deeply troubled lives who were completely changed through faith in Jesus Christ—alcoholics (some of whom had tried eighteen different cures), drug addicts, homosexuals, and moral, decent people whose lives were so bound by fear they couldn't step outside their homes. Disciplines that fail to recognize humanity's essential spiritual nature are bound to be impotent when it comes to treating the maladies of the spirit.

When we have stepped outside of the will of God, we have a spiritual problem. The answer is to deal with the problem as what it really is—sin. Only then can we get back into harmony with the Father's will.

The life of Jonah the prophet has been reproduced in the lives of millions of men and women who went to church as children but "outgrew" their faith in their teen years or in college. They turned their backs on God and lived as though He did not exist, as though they were not accountable to Him, and as though eternity did not exist. Like Jonah, their problem is spiritual. They are out of the will of God for their lives. The result (in Jonah's words): "My soul fainted within me" (Jonah 2:7). That was Jonah's spiritual problem. The physical one may have been high blood pressure that threatened to blow off the top of his head. But giving Jonah little white pills for blood pressure wouldn't have been what he needed. Only repentance, confession, and striking out in a new direction could solve his problem.

Undiagnosed and ignored, spiritual afflictions result in emotional suffering and even physical pain. The apostle Paul recognized this in the Corinthian church: "Many are weak and sick among you, and many sleep [are dead]" (1 Corinthians 11:30).

Dr. Jack Kelly, one of Scotland's finest cardiologists, was once talking with me about the emotional and spiritual needs of people. He related how on one occasion he had been asked to examine a patient who was suffering with "heart pains." He found no physical malady. Being a dedicated believer, however, he began to question his patient further, only to discover that the patient had recently returned from Paris and was suffering an acute case of guilt because of sexual misconduct. Although most cardiologists' skill runs out when the electrocardiogram looks normal, Jack Kelly knew how to treat both problems.

The answer to spiritual guilt lies in applying the resources of forgiveness and cleansing through the blood of Jesus Christ, a solution that you can prescribe freely as a layman.

When Larry Crabb finished his doctoral program in clinical psychology, he had divided the problems of people into two categories: "emotional problems" and "spiritual problems." Speaking of that division, Crabb says, "I regarded the resources of Christianity as welcome additions to the Christian therapist's little black bag of techniques. However, I distinguished clearly between psychological problems and spiritual problems. For solving psychological problems, I believed that Christianity was often helpful but rarely essential."[1]

However, as Crabb began to work with people, he discovered that people often came to him complaining of surface problems. But when he began to work with them, he couldn't put his finger on any substantial problem. He says, "Probing more deeply, I noticed that this person had a lot of foolish ideas about life that took no real account of God and that he or she had a stubborn inclination to do wrong and an equally stubborn unwillingness to admit being wrong."[2]

At that point Crabb realized he was dealing with problems that couldn't really be labeled as "mental disease" but rather "required far more than psychology could offer." Instead of considering Christianity to be something that was "helpful but not essential," Crabb began to see it as "essential in solving personal problems"; a personal relationship with Christ, he realized, was "a necessary foundation for dealing with all problems, psychological or spiritual."[3]

Guiding a person into the will of God means "deprogramming" a lot of the ideas that have permeated our society, such as:

- My fulfillment is the most important thing in the world.
- My happiness is imperative.
- Enough money would solve any problem.
- Someone else could probably better meet my needs.
- Sex may not be everything in life, but it's way ahead of whatever is in second place.
- If I were only more beautiful, I would be loved.
- If you really loved me, you would know what I think.

In the secular world, believers are bombarded by philosophies and ideologies that run counter to God's plan and purpose for their lives. At the same time, our sinful nature constantly wars against God's plan for our lives.

If the person who came to you for help fully saw this and understood the implications of his past actions, he probably would not be faced with his present difficulties. Recognizing the cause, however, will help him arrive at a solution.

BE A GOOD LISTENER

Another failure that results in improper diagnosis is not hearing what the person you are helping is really saying. Your communication skills are important, and if they are lacking, you can develop them. Obviously, you can't be listening at the same time your mind is going ahead of what the person is saying. Neither can you listen very well if you are thinking about the responsibilities you carry and how you really ought to be doing something other than listening to the person who hurts. Take time, listen, pray, and evaluate, and only then will you be ready to respond to the question, "What do you think I should do?"

I will talk about diagnosing the emotional aspects of a person in chapter 8, which is devoted to counseling people with emotional problems from a biblical perspective. But first, in the next chapter, I want to examine the difference between counseling from a biblical perspective and counseling from a secular perspective.

QUESTIONS FOR
THOUGHT AND DISCUSSION

1. Can you think of an example in your own life when a physical problem had emotional symptoms (or vice versa)? Did this have any effect on your spiritual life as well?

2. The word "holy" has the same word root as "healthy" and "whole." How do you think this applies to the healing God wants for us as whole people (body, mind, and spirit)?

3. Why is listening so important to the counseling process?

CHAPTER 6

COUNSELING "BY THE BOOK" OR BY *THE* BOOK?

(HOW SECULAR AND BIBLICAL COUNSELING DIFFER)

An experiment was conducted recently by psychologists at Vanderbilt University who wanted to know if the advice of untrained, nonprofessionals who were warm and cordial was as effective as that of trained psychotherapists. The group of professionals, some of the best in their area, had an average of twenty-three years of experience behind them. The second group were college professors who had no formal experience or training in counseling.

Both groups worked with troubled people for no more than twenty-five hours, and at the end of that time comparisons were made. The results: "Patients undergoing psychotherapy with college professors showed. . .quantitatively as much improvement as patients treated by experienced professional psychotherapists."[1]

In an unrelated article, the *Washington Post*'s magazine, *Insight,* decries the impotence of psychoanalysis, saying, "Were surgeons to have the same cure rate as psychoanalysts, there would be no surgery; they would all be in prison on malpractice charges."[2]

There is probably less agreement among professionals in the field of psychiatry as to what really works than there is in any other scientific discipline.

Psychiatrist Garth Wood, in his book *The Myth of Neurosis: Overcoming the Illness Excuse*, breaks with the traditions of his profession, arguing that untrained professionals are some of the best sources of help for people.[3] He's convinced that a person who has an intimate knowledge of another person can be a powerful force for good. After all, friends know each other's strengths and weaknesses; they know each other's habit patterns, personal idiosyncrasies, and motivations. Friends start out with an edge that the professional can gain only after hours of conversation and prodding.

Those of you who know Christ as your personal Lord and Savior have an additional source of wisdom and insight: the indwelling presence of the Holy Spirit. During Passion Week, Jesus spoke of the coming Holy Spirit four times.[4] He used a term that had not previously been used for the Holy Spirit, *parakletos,* a word that English versions of the Bible translate as "Counselor." Jesus told the disciples that He would ask the Father to send them another Counselor, who would guide them into truth and show them things to come. This is the same One who indwells the child of God today, giving insights and direction.

Perhaps you are asking, "Do you really believe that?" Yes, I am convinced, on the basis of my own experience, that the Holy Spirit will help you pick up on things that people say, things you would otherwise have overlooked, that will lead the conversation directly to vital issues. "It just happens!" you may protest, but I don't think so. God knows the future; He also knows the past in ways that you do not, and as you counsel, He will prompt you to ask questions and give you new insights. The Holy Spirit serves as the Counselor who guides you, at the same time that He helps the person you counsel move into the will of God.

THE HOLY SPIRIT AND COUNSELING

The Holy Spirit, the third Person of the Trinity, is holy because holiness is part of the nature of God. Behind the word "holy" are two concepts: purity and separation. The Holy Spirit is not an abstract or a philosophical idea, but a Person with the will and the mind of God. He brings conviction. He guides us into truth. He is the agent of conversion; and when it comes to counseling, He is the source of lasting personality change, as our old nature gives way to Christlikeness.

For centuries, people have debated the issue of nature versus nurture—heredity versus environment; this controversy matters little when the Holy Spirit begins to work in a life, a process the New Testament describes as "sanctification." Three times the Bible tells us that this work of "knocking off the rough edges" of our old nature is the work of God's Holy Spirit.[5]

In the first century, to call a person a "Corinthian" slurred that person's character and morality. People who lived in this ancient city didn't boast of their family heritage, as did the Athenians. Crowning the acropolis overlooking the city was the grand temple of Aphrodite, the goddess of sexuality, whose one thousand priestesses were merely glorified prostitutes. Adulterers, homosexuals, transvestites, alcoholics, extortioners, and perverts were among those mentioned by Paul in his letter to the Corinthians. But after this list Paul says, "And such were some of you. . . . But you were sanctified. . .by the Spirit of our God" (1 Corinthians 6:11).

This grand work of sanctification by God's Holy Spirit is something that cannot be understood or duplicated in the secular world. It is the victory of the Spirit over both heredity and environment.

The Holy Spirit works through the agency of men and women who are in touch with Him—which means God uses you as you help people work through their problems. In his book *Competent to Counsel,* Jay Adams says, "The use of human agency in counseling. . .does not in itself bypass the work of the Spirit, to the contrary, it is the principal and ordinary means by which He works."[6] In other words, God, through the agency of His Spirit, works in and through us to bring people into conformity with His will. You have an important part to play in restoring order to the kingdom of God, the order that was lost when sin made its dark entrance into the world. This is why you need to work in harmony with the Holy Spirit, not against Him, as you guide people toward the will of God.

Some may ask, "Why not use the Bible in conjunction with some of the modern techniques of psychology?" After all, many techniques are amoral; that is, they are neither good nor evil in themselves.

We *can* learn something from these secular disciplines—but far too often, without realizing it, we adopt secular frameworks of counseling rather than working from the gospel's foundation. As we discussed in an earlier chapter, Christian counseling requires a radical shift in our outlook. I believe we need to start with this radical shift and work from there, rather than the other way around. Use the gospel as your starting point and incorporate a few secular techniques if need be—but don't try to start from a secular technique and then incorporate a few Bible verses here and there. If you do, you are not truly counseling from a Christian perspective, but rather a secular one that has been sprinkled with Scripture.

In his book *Psychological Seduction*, William Kirk Kilpatrick says:

> *True Christianity does not mix well with psychology. When you try to mix them, you often end up with a watered-down Christianity*

instead of a Christianized psychology. But the
process is subtle and is rarely noticed. I wasn't
aware that I was confusing two different
things. And others in the church who might
have been expected to put me right were under
the same enchantment as I. It was not a
frontal attack on Christianity—I'm sure I
would have resisted that. It was not a case of a
wolf at the door—the wolf was already in the
fold, dressed in sheep's clothing. And from the
way it was petted and fed by some of the shep-
herds, one would think it was the prize sheep.[7]

How Do People Get So Confused?

Often people find themselves in positions of spiritual leadership through no decision of their own. They don't ask to be counselors; it just happens because they are Bible teachers, leaders of discussion groups, or outgoing persons to whom others are readily attracted. Others begin to look to them for guidance and help.

God blesses their efforts with modest success, but sometimes they struggle with inadequacies. They often think, *I could help people a lot more if I had some training.* Uncertain of where or how to get that training, these individuals may enroll in a secular psychology course or a course in counseling at a local university.

I have known some people with Bible school or seminary training who then took secular training in counseling—and didn't even recognize that the methods they learned violated scriptural principles. Apparently, they had a huge blind spot when it came to integrating the two points of view; they never even noticed how totally at odds the two perspectives were. Somehow, they managed to practice both. Others, however, were overwhelmed by the secular assault on their faith—and their faith went right out the window.

Alex was like that. He grew up in the church, went to seminary, and then became a pastor who had a real heart for people. As the counseling load grew, he realized that he needed more tools. Feeling that he could better help people if he were a psychiatrist, Alex gave up his church, enrolled in medical school at Berkeley, and became a psychiatrist.

By the time he finished his work in psychiatry, Alex, to the great regret and confusion of his family and friends, gave up his faith. Today he no longer attends church or believes in God. "Anything you want to believe is fine if it works," he tells his clients.

For far too long, we who are evangelicals have had an intellectual inferiority complex; we assume the secular world has a corner on knowledge that we don't have. "If we are really going to find acceptance in the world," we reason, "we had better take the best of what the gospel has to offer and cloak it with secular intellectualism."

This complex is an old one. Remember that the

children of Israel wanted a king to be "like all the nations" (see 1 Samuel 8:5, 20). "They have not rejected you," God told Samuel, "but they have rejected Me" (1 Samuel 8–7). Their desire for a king resulted in bondage. Anytime we desire something that is outside of the plan and purpose of God, we may get it—but we pay the price of bondage to have it. It isn't that some non-Christian professors aren't intelligent; it's simply that they "know" so many things that are in violation of God's guidelines. Both simply cannot be true.

How Secular Counseling Models Differ from the Biblical Model

At the risk of oversimplification, I'd like to point out that there are three basic secular models used in counseling today, and they all differ dramatically from the biblical model I have presented. The moral model comes the closest to it, but it still offers no absolutes; instead, it holds a subjective concept of ethics that is different for different people.

Freudian Model
Root of the Problem: Victim of Conscience
or Environment
Cure: Psychoanalysis (six to eight years)

MEDICAL MODEL
> *Root of the Problem:* Victim of Chemistry;
>   Mental Illness (like a virus from without)
> *Cure:* Psychotherapy Drugs

MORAL MODEL
> *Root of the Problem:* Violator of Morality
>   (standards too high)
> *Cure:* Psychotherapy (talking cures)

BIBLICAL MODEL
> *Root of the Problem:* Violator of will of God
> *Cure:* Confession, Repentance, Restoration,
>   Restitution

Another approach would be to contrast the major premises of secular disciplines with the biblical model.

SECULAR MODELS
1. Follow the ground rules of the school's founder such as Freud, Mowrer, Adler, Jung, or whoever.
2. Are human-centered or client-centered, thus God is unimportant.
3. Struggle with lack of clearly defined areas of responsibility.
4. Offer no lasting hope that life will be different.
5. Often end in failure and may result in further despair and bondage.

BIBLICAL ALTERNATIVES
1. Follow the principles of Scripture.
2. Relate humans to God and thus accept scriptural guidelines for interpersonal relations.
3. Human beings are responsible and can change. Recognize sin and forgiveness.
4. Changed character promises the hope of a better future.
5. Lead to change.

Have I been too hard on secular disciplines? I am not suggesting that all non-Christian counselors have nothing to offer—but I *am* saying that philosophical models that leave God out do not offer solutions that go to the heart of human problems. Humanity's deepest troubles all stem from areas where we have gone outside the will of God.

Some people, who basically follow the moral model, have indeed helped many people. They come close to the biblical model of counseling, but they stop just short of what the Bible actually says about responsibility and grace. For example, Dr. Thomas Szasz, sometimes called the "anti-psychiatric psychiatrist," has for many years criticized the irresponsibility of psychoanalysis, which he considers to be an endless search to hang responsibility on something or someone else. And he is not alone. For at least twenty years before his death in 1983, O. Hobart Mowrer denounced the psychoanalytic theories of

Freud. He called for increasing the power of conscience, and spoke of "a very present hell on this earth, the hell to which unexpiated sin and guilt lead us."

More recently, Garth Wood, the outspoken critic of psychiatry (who, don't forget, is himself a psychiatrist), alleges that far too much credence has been given to the idea that people suffer from a disease that we call "neurosis," just as people suffer from mumps or pneumonia. He contends that the medical model of mental illness (you are attacked by mental illness just as you would get a cold or the flu) has little, if any, validity. Neurosis is a myth, he says. Wood believes that psychological cure comes through first admitting wrongdoing, and then through atonement: doing something that rectifies the wrong and thereby leads to mental health. Yet Wood still stops short of biblical truth. Fuller Seminary professor H. Newton Malony, in reviewing his book, charges that Wood "seems far less interested in what is right than in what will work."[8]

The contrast between the mentality of the secular person and the individual in whom dwells the Spirit of God is nothing new. Paul experienced this discrepancy in Corinth as he tried to communicate the difference that a personal knowledge of Jesus Christ really makes. Almost as though he were giving up trying to relate to the secular mind, he says, "The natural man does not receive the things of the Spirit of God, for they are foolishness to him; nor can he know them, because they are spiritually discerned" (1 Corinthians 2:14).

What difference does this Christian mind-set make as we strive to help people?

COUNSELING IN COOPERATION WITH THE SPIRIT OF GOD

Biblical Counseling is God-Centered

Most secular counseling is human-centered and deals with "felt needs." The temptation for the Christian who has been trained in a secular environment is to keep humanity at the center and bring God into the picture in such a way that He becomes a spiritual "Band-Aid" to get us off the hook when we are in trouble.

The whole focus is wrong! Apart from a relationship with God, there will never be enough pieces to fit the puzzle of life's problems together. This is why Jesus Christ came. God's plan is to bring us into harmony with His divine will and thus to change our natures through the new birth.

As long as our thinking is fuzzy in this regard, we will never see the larger picture, and our image of God will only be a reflection of our own natures. Our God will be too small!

Biblical Counseling Recognizes
the Sinfulness of Human Nature

This does not imply that anyone who struggles with a problem is suffering from sin, but it does recognize that most of the problems necessitating counseling are the direct or indirect result of our sinful nature. Notice the catalog of the characteristics of the flesh (our sinful nature) recorded in Galatians 5:19–21: "adultery, fornication, uncleanness, lewdness, idolatry, sorcery, hatred, contentions [arguments], jealousies, outbursts of wrath, selfish ambitions, dissensions, heresies, envy, murders, drunkenness, revelries, and the like." These are the same factors that still create unhappiness today.

When the Bible says, "For all have sinned and fall short of the glory of God," and "There is none righteous, no, not one" (Romans 3:23,10), we clearly see that even in the best of people are the incipient dregs of rottenness that are found in the worst of people. (But, by the same token, in even the worst people are certain qualities that reflect the fact that human beings were made in the image of the divine.)

Have you ever had the experience of going to your garden to till the soil and finding a boulder or an old rotten board that had to be moved? As you picked it up, dozens, possibly hundreds, of creeping, crawling bugs and slugs began to squirm. Well, imagine that is what we dredge up from the recesses of our hearts, the dark corners where our old selfish natures lurk. Speaking of the heart as the seat of our affections and choices, Jeremiah wrote, "The heart is deceitful above all things, and desperately wicked; who can know it?" (Jeremiah 17:9).

How else can we explain the humiliating and devastating consequences that have followed the poor choices some Christians have made, choices that resulted in actions totally out of character with the lives they had lived over the years? To their dying days, these people will regret the decisions they made—and yet their actions merely embodied the sordid thoughts within their hearts. None of us is immune from the same mistake. Paul warns, "Therefore let him who thinks he stands take heed lest he fall" (1 Corinthians 10:12).

This book isn't intended to be theological, so I won't attempt an exhaustive treatment of sin, but I need to point out that Isaiah 53:6 gives a clear picture of what sin does in relationship to the will of God. It leads us astray from the right path, and the end result is unhappiness.

Biblical counseling recognizes that all people sin because of the pull of their old sinful natures, as well as because of their personal choices. That's why none of us can say, "I'm not responsible; I couldn't help it!" We sin by nature and by choice. We end up with problems that we just can't handle without outside help.

Discouragement and despair characterize the mentally ill, people who have struggled with their problems month after month, in some cases year after year. If you tell people that their behavior is perfectly normal and that they must simply learn to accept it, you sentence them to a life of perpetual despair.

Suppose you went to a dentist with a toothache, and he took a look at your abscessed gum and said, "Hmm, that tooth doesn't look very good, but, friend, there's nothing to worry about. Everybody here is troubled with this kind of problem. The great solution is acceptance and understanding." If somebody told you that, you would get another dentist—and fast!

So when you tell someone, "Look, your problem is sin! But there is an answer to this problem!" your counsel is neither cruel nor devastating. It defines the true malady and offers a real solution. Though sin is a spiritual problem, our emotions, our relationships, and our self-concepts are all affected. Sin throws all of our beings out of whack.

Notice how different are these secular approaches to people's problems:

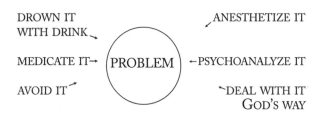

DROWN IT WITH DRINK

ANESTHETIZE IT

MEDICATE IT → PROBLEM ← PSYCHOANALYZE IT

AVOID IT

DEAL WITH IT GOD'S WAY

Counseling from a secular perspective masks sin

as a "sickness" that can be medicated, lived with, or removed. Your job as a counselor-friend is not that of a surgeon who removes the problem; instead, you are the one who holds the flashlight so the person can see the problem. But God's Spirit performs the surgery.

My son and I had backpacked high into the Sierras to enjoy the magnificent scenery and get away from civilization. While we were fishing in some of the high lakes, Steve's fly line somehow backlashed, sinking the barbed hook deeply into his hand. Calmly, he walked over to me and said, "Dad, I've got a problem."

After he showed me, we walked back to camp, considering the options we had. The first was to break camp, hike down the mountain, and find a doctor who could do the appropriate surgery to remove the hook. We didn't much like the idea of giving up the rest of our trip, so we began to look for other options.

"What do we have that could help us get this thing out?"

When I had exhausted my inventory of ideas, Steve asked, "Dad, do you have a new double-edged razor blade in your pack?"

I had one. I sterilized it; then, with a steady hand, Steve calmly performed surgery on himself and removed that unwanted fishhook! He had found his own solution.

Your task as a biblical counselor isn't to say, "Boy, that was a dumb thing you did!" (Who in their right mind would sink a fishing hook into their hand miles from civilization?) In dealing with problems that have taken people outside the will of God, you don't have to berate people or condemn them. Instead, your job is to offer support and help the other person find the right solution. Help them identify the problem, so that they can correct it by following the next guideline.

Biblical Counseling Follows the Principles of God's Word, the Bible

The Bible offers sound counsel when it comes to the issues of life. I am convinced that one of the greatest needs of people today is to understand what the Bible says about handling problems that cause what we describe as mental illness. Few people who fill the pews of churches today understand what it really means to be forgiven, to be adopted as a child of God and brought into the family of God. Having never been confronted with the sovereignty of God, they are overly concerned with the multitude of worries that drive them into the asphalt. Not understanding the will of God, they struggle, often against Him, trying to achieve things that are not really in their best interests. Inevitably, this leads to mental stress.

Many of the situations that cause people to reach out to others for guidance are situations that merely necessitate decisions of one kind or another. We live in a world of stress and confusion, and at times we all need someone to simply say, "Look, you are on the right track; keep moving." We need someone to reinforce what we already feel is the will of God for our lives. Or we need someone to help us find what His will is.

At other times, however, we assume workloads and burdens that exceed our capacity to handle them. Sometimes I illustrate this truth by pointing to the podium or the table that holds my speaking notes and asking, "How many of you think I could stand on this table?"

Those who are still awake raise their hands.

Then I ask, "If I stand on this and have a couple more people stand on it, how many think it will support us?" Obviously, the stress increases in direct proportion to the weight on the top, and at some point the structure will collapse. Our lives are the same way.

Another illustration I often use is that of fish swimming in a pond. When a fisherman comes along, hooks one of the fish, and pulls, the fish begins to swim erratically, flopping back and forth in the water as more pressure is exerted by the fisherman. Other fish swimming in the pond think, "He really looks crazy—look at all the funny gyrations our brother fish is going through."

In a similar way, the more pressure some of us face, the greater our need for someone to relieve the pressure causing our erratic behavior. That's when a counselor becomes important.

Dr. Karl Menninger illustrated sanity and

insanity as being on two opposite ends of a line forming a continuum:

SANITY	INSANITY
ABILITY TO FUNCTION	THE INABILITY TO FUNCTION

Menninger contended that everyone moves back and forth on this continuum. On some days you feel completely in control; on other days you feel driven and pushed by your schedule, at the mercy of your emotions—and you don't like it. When you reach the point where you are no longer able to function, you need help.

Vast resources in the Bible can be brought to bear on our personal needs (see chapter 8 for specific Scriptures that deal with such problems as worry and fear). The greater our knowledge of God's plan for our lives, the less we will need counseling from some other individual. We will be able to go instead directly to the source of all help and health.

One of the greatest services a pastor can do for the congregation's mental health is not necessarily to spend long hours in counseling (which is important), but to faithfully teach and proclaim the Word. As the congregation gains knowledge of the Bible, the pastor will usually discover that most of the people who need counseling are coming from outside the church. They will not be the people who sit in the congregation Sunday after Sunday, soaking up the Word.

You who are involved in study groups (whether you are a teacher, a discussion leader, or merely set up chairs for the meeting) are on the front lines of building solid lives and contributing to good mental health. You're doing preventative therapy!

Biblical Counseling Results in Liberation, Not Further Bondage

There is no frustration as great as that suffered by a person who has gone from psychiatrist to psychiatrist, hoping for help, only to be told that nothing can be done. To describe a person's problem as a "sickness" that can only be medicated, or at best suppressed, offers no hope that life can be different. William, who had been under the care of a psychiatrist for nineteen years, felt this sort of despair.

As I sat down that first afternoon and listened to William and his wife pour out their hearts, I sensed that the greatest need in their lives was for a personal relationship with Jesus Christ. Though I seldom share the plan of salvation on anyone's first visit, this time I opened my Bible and explained how God loved us so much that He sent His Son to be our Savior. When we receive Him as Lord and Master, I told them, we become new persons in Christ Jesus.

When William returned the following week, he reported that he had never been so happy as he had been that week. Part of his difficulty had always been an unresolved problem of guilt, which could never be tranquilized completely. When he turned to Christ, however, that sense of guilt began to dissipate. I began working with William, applying biblical principles to the needs of his life.

Now I could move on to step number two: Get William to a doctor who would begin to decrease his daily dosage of tranquilizers, and supervise an exercise program. I remembered that when I met William for a morning walk that first week, he seemed to plod, barely able to get one foot in front of the other. The decrease in tranquilizers began to let his body's natural energies take over, and after a few weeks, he was completely free of drugs. As a result, he was a new man with a new marriage. Spiritual freedom led naturally to physical and emotional freedom as well.

"For to be carnally minded is death, but to be spiritually minded is life and peace" (Romans 8:6). God's principles really work!

Before we go on to a new chapter, I want to suggest some guidelines for using Scripture in counseling. The way you use the Bible has a great deal to do with the way God's Holy Spirit interacts with the person you are trying to help. You either help or hinder, depending on how you use the Word.

Suggestions for Handling
Scripture More Effectively

Don't Thump 'Em with a Bible Verse
as Soon as You Hear What's Going On

Scores of people do this. *I know what your problem is,* you think to yourself, *and here's the solution.*

Just a minute, you may be thinking, *isn't that what biblical counseling is about?* Hebrews 4:12 says, "The word of God is living and active. Sharper than any double-edged sword, it penetrates even to dividing soul and spirit, joints and marrow; it judges the thoughts and attitudes of the heart" (NIV).

Yes, God's word is powerful. But it can be misused. Only the ministry of God's Holy Spirit can take the Word and speak to a human heart, convicting, reproving, and bringing a person to the point of decision and commitment. When we pick up the Bible like a club, we only anger our friends and make them run the other way. Don't try to do the Holy Spirit's job. If we try to use the Word with our own powers, we will inevitably fail.

Use the Word as a Mirror

In moving from the encounter phase of counseling to the reconstruction phase, you must bring the person into confrontation with God and His will. Instead of using the Bible as a club, use it as a mirror, helping your friend see himself as God sees him. The Greek word that is translated "to confess" literally means "to say the same thing"; when we acknowledge wrong-doing before God, we are in reality saying what God says. We look into the Bible's mirror, and we see ourselves just as God sees us.

Let's suppose a friend is telling you that she is considering walking away from a marriage. She explains that she is tired of earning the major part of the living and that she's had it—she's going to file for divorce. You can respond, "Don't you know God hates broken homes and living with someone else makes you an adulterer?" But your friend already knows that, and your shocked response will only drive her away. Maybe instead you might say, "Have you ever done a study of what the Bible says about expectations in marriage and how we should respond to them?" The answer this time will probably be, "No—I haven't." This in turn opens the door for you to say, "Would you be interested in joining me and we'll do a study together?"

In the process, your friend will not only see that her course of action doesn't measure up to God's standards, but she will also gain hope that things can be different. As the counselor, you will have the opportunity to suggest a variety of other solutions to her problem.

Use the Bible as Medicine for the Soul;
God's Word Can Heal the Brokenness of Our Lives

Our culture teaches us that we have to look after

ourselves first. As a result, all too many people live life with the mental attitudes of scavengers on the streets, when they could live like people who owned a penthouse. As counselors, this is where we have to be willing to depart from the standards of our culture. When we do, we can show how lives can be different through a real encounter with God, through appropriating His grace to our lives. God's Word is the vehicle, the channel of blessing.

When you are counseling a friend, you may need to help her believe that the promises of God have her name attached. At times I will suggest to someone, "In place of the word 'whoever' or 'anyone' in the Scripture passage, insert your name. This promise has your name attached to it." (For example, "God so loved *Mary* that he gave his one and only Son, so that if *Mary* believes in him, *Mary* shall not perish but have eternal life" [adapted from John 3:16 NIV].)

People today are looking for solutions, and that is exactly what the Bible offers. Use God's Word with the surgeon's skill, wielding it so deftly that healing takes place.

Now let's go on to apply what we have just talked about to real-life situations. The next three chapters will help you use the Bible to deal with problems with relationships, problems of the emotions, and problems relating to addictive behavior. I do not intend for them to be in-depth studies, but guides that can be applied to a wide spectrum of issues.

QUESTIONS FOR THOUGHT AND DISCUSSION

1. Jesus used the word "Counselor" for the Holy Spirit. As men and women dedicated to being effective in helping friends who have needs, how can we allow the Holy Spirit to work through us?

2. What do you think a Christian's attitude should be toward secular psychology?

3. Why do you think some people lose their faith in Christ when they enroll in secular psychology programs?

4. Why is the concept of sin essential to the Christian counselor?

5. Do you think a belief in sin makes a Christian counselor more positive in her approach or more negative? Why?

6. Can you think of any other ways (besides the ones given by Dr. Sala) that the Bible could be used more effectively by Christian counselors?

CHAPTER 7

USING THE BIBLE TO COUNSEL RELATIONSHIP PROBLEMS

Many of the problems that bring people to you for counseling are the results of missing God's plan. A person traveling from San Francisco to New York may have successfully traversed the highways for two thousand miles (like a person with twenty-five good years of marriage), yet if he takes a wrong turn in Chicago (perhaps betraying his spouse), he may eventually end up in Toronto (or with a broken home). Having taken wrong turns, having made poor choices, at times having sinned, he has to re-adjust his paths and take new directions.

Everything that happens within the confines of a home affects all the members of that family because a family is an intricate pattern of relationships. Not surprisingly, then, much of our counseling involves relationships, especially relationships within families. In a family of four, at least sixteen separate relationships exist, the relationships of each person to the other three as well as the individual relationships (how they each feel about themselves); all these relationships affect emotional health and happiness. No wonder family living is complex.

Illnesses, career reversals, accidents, financial problems, the birth or death of a child, even aging that changes our appearance and outlook, all these are part of the tapestry of relationships. These events generally have nothing to do with personal failure, nor are they the result of individual sin, but nonetheless, they are issues that often require counseling and support.

As I read the letters of the thousands of men and women who listen to our *Guidelines* radio program and then write for personal help, I've discovered that we can never assume that believers in Jesus Christ, even when they are involved in a church, have a very deep knowledge of Scripture. This fact means that you can't take anything for granted; you have to use the Word, showing people directly what God's perspective is and how it is different from ours.

The application of God's Word is a positive thing that gives hope in a broken world. It takes away the despair of those who see no way out of their situation. It allows a broken person to see light at the end of a dark tunnel. And it leads to the healing of our relationships with others.

At times, the people you help will have grown up with a clear knowledge of right and wrong. They may not always do the right thing, but at least they know what it is. A growing number of people, though, especially those under age forty, have been raised by permissive parents in homes that had fuzzy ideas about right and wrong. By the same token, our role models and heroes today are often individuals whose integrity is tainted. They seem to be admired more because of what they do (or get away with) than because of who they are.

"Integrity," says Ted Engstrom in his book by the same title, "simply put. . .is doing what you said you would do."[1] This sort of integrity is all too absent in our world today; but where it does exist, it has an enormous impact on our relationships. When it comes to marriage, it includes a monogamous commitment. In the family, integrity leads to loyalty and trustworthiness. In friendships, it means support and acceptance.

But when people don't do what they said they would do, or what the other person thinks they said they would do, conflict results. Relationships are broken. At times broken relationships are caused by unkept promises. Other times they are the result of wrong choices that damage relationships, and sometimes they happen because of misunderstandings or different points of view, which have to be reconciled through better communication and understanding.

In chapter 4, I said one of the goals of counseling is to help your friend see himself or herself as he or she really is. Another goal is to help your friend see the situation from a mate's viewpoint (or the viewpoint of the person with whom there is conflict). A third goal, and most important of all, is for your friend to see the issue from God's perspective, which then gives the motivation necessary to initiate changes that will result in forgiveness and the restoration of broken relationships.

Clear communication is vital for resolving broken relationships. Every time a person makes a statement there are three components:

> What you said (the face value of the
> statement)
> What you meant to say (which may not be
> what you actually said)
> What you implied (which you may not have
> actually said at all)

When we were living in Manila, Philippines, I took my twelve-year-old son to an exotic bird farm to take pictures of the rare and unusual birds. Both of us were photographing the birds, when a peacock began to spread his tail feathers. I reached for my camera and said, "Get one!"—meaning, "Get a picture of the bird."

But Steve immediately lunged for the tail feathers of the bird, intending to pull one out. "No, Steve!" I yelled. "That's not what I meant."

"But, Dad, you said, 'Get one!' "

"Yes, but I meant 'Get a picture!' "

Here's how the misunderstanding happened:

> I said, "Get one."
> I meant, "Get a picture."
> I implied, "Get a tail feather."

Communication broke down!

Jesus said, "Therefore, whatever you want men to do to you, do also to them. . ." (Matthew 7:12). This means that we must also communicate with others in the way we would want them to communicate with us. To do that, we must also be willing to clear up the misunderstandings that result when communication breaks down through no fault of our own.

John was on a business trip, and while he was away Mary spent hours on the phone talking to travel agents, airline reservation clerks, waiting, taking notes, getting the best deal for their summer vacation. Wanting to clear the plans with her husband before she ordered nonrefundable, no-change tickets, Mary called his office and left a message for him to return her call after dinner. But John didn't get the message.

An errant secretary finally remembered the next morning and interrupted a business meeting with the message to call home immediately. John did and became angry and brusque because he had been called out of a meeting to hear about next summer's vacation. And Mary, who had no intention of interrupting a business meeting, felt that he was angry with her without cause. She was miffed that he cared so little about her hard work.

John didn't know that Mary had called the previous day. Mary didn't realize that John was interrupted in a business meeting. Reconstructing the actual situation, both realized that they were blaming the other for something neither had intended. Clear communication and understanding helped them resolve the issue.

A FRAMEWORK FOR BIBLICAL COUNSELING

The following points are matters that you as a counselor need to resolve firmly in your thinking before you even begin to help others work through relationship problems.

God is a Good God; Therefore,
What He Tells Us in His Word Is
His Plan for Healthy Relationships

Of course, this cuts across the grain of secular images that picture God as a bully, a cosmic Policeman out to get you when you are bad, or the Great Enforcer whose black Book (the Bible) was designed to make you miserable. Another version of this secular thinking is that the Bible may be well and good, but it is only the fantasy of old men with long gray beards who wrote it long ago.

In reality, however, the Bible is full of practical, life-giving advice that can be applied to any relationship today. When you counsel from a biblical perspective, you use the Bible to enlighten, to guide, and to encourage as well as to reprove and censure (when necessary). But the end goal is for people to be able to live in peace and harmony with those they love.

Healing Broken Relationships
Instead of Dissolving Them
Is Working in Harmony with God's Plan

God knows how we are made (after all, He made us!), and He understands that inevitably, we will have conflicts in our relationships. He could not be a good God if He had not given us the means to resolve those conflicts.

The conflicts that destroy relationships today are not new. Infidelity, broken promises, and misunderstandings produce hostility and anger, jealousy and deceit. All of these are pictured in the lives of those whose stories are told in the Bible.

Anyone who thinks we should have no conflicts in our relationships are being about as realistic as if they expected all Christian wives to be a combination of Mother Teresa, Betty Crocker, and Farrah Fawcett—or all Christian husbands to walk on water and leap over buildings in a single bound.

When two people come together in marriage, they "become one flesh," in the words of Scripture—but their union in marriage doesn't mean the instant, perfect bonding of their emotions or personality traits. Every person is a collage of customs, emotions, family traditions, idiosyncrasies, and personalities. The process of "becoming one" weaves all these different ingredients into the tapestry of a new relationship. This will eventually form the fabric of a new family. But the process is hard work; it involves conflict and real struggle. Resolving this conflict is one part of Christ's healing ministry.

Some Conflicts Are Not Caused by Personal Failure but Are the Result of Living in a Broken World

I've noticed a widespread belief that just won't go away: "If what happens to me is good, it's obvious that God is blessing me; and if it's bad, it's the judgment of God or the devil who did it." However, nowhere does the Bible support this belief.

"Why was my baby born with five holes in her heart? Is God punishing her for what I did?" Those were the questions of a young mother I met. Before I could say anything, Susan began to unload the pent-up emotions of her heart. She had grown up in a home where her parents were strict disciplinarians. When she became a teenager, she rebelled and sowed her share of defiant wild oats. She refused to listen to her parent's stern admonition that "God's going to punish you for what you are doing!"

Then one day shortly after she married, she was walking down the street and heard music drifting through the open windows of a church. She stopped to listen and finally entered. That day, Susan gave her heart to the Lord and became a Christian. Nonetheless, her parents' words kept hammering her conscience: *God's going to get you for what you've done!*

A series of calamities befell the young married couple, but I don't believe any of them were the judgment of God or the result of satanic attack. A flood destroyed their apartment and they lost the wedding gifts friends had given them. Their first child was stillborn, and now their little baby had been born with five tiny holes in her heart and was not expected to live beyond age two. Their relationship with their child would apparently soon be broken by death.

But this young mother was not to blame. We live in an imperfect world. That means we are not personally responsible for each broken relationship that confronts us. People will ask, "Why did God let this happen to me? Why did He fail me? Why is He punishing me? What did I do?" When that happens, you will have to answer, "God did not fail you—your husband failed you" or "your wife failed you!"

At times, though, as in Susan's case, there's no person we can blame. You can go crazy trying to come up with an adequate explanation for some situations. In this life, we may never know the answer to our "whys." As counselors, then, we need to shift the focus elsewhere. Rather than concentrating on finding an answer, we can help the hurting person realize God will meet us at the point of our deepest needs.

Consider, for example, the woman who suspects her husband is unfaithful to her, and yet she desperately needs his income to care for their seven children. Or imagine the plight of an aged widow whose support comes from a son stricken with an incurable disease, or the husband who struggles with guilt because he allowed doctors to perform surgery that resulted in his wife's death. What of the wife who has forgiven her husband for his affair, yet has to cope with diminished income because he must also support the child who was born of infidelity? All of these people can be overwhelmed with the question "Why?" It can immobilize them so that they are unable to move forward in life. However, if instead they turn to Christ, finding His presence even in the midst of their deepest pain, they will find that He will heal their broken hearts. They don't need to know "why"; they need to know the Savior.

Some situations—caused by living in a broken world—cannot be resolved. Learning to cope with these situations is part of the healing process. To bear anger or bitterness toward another or toward God can destroy lives. Through counseling, you help your friend forgive those who have brought pain and grief and understand that God was not the One who failed. You help her see God as a refuge in times of trouble (Nahum 1:7 NIV), a hiding place in times of distress (Psalms 32:7; 119:114). God will help her cope with what cannot be changed.

God Promised to Be With Us in Times of Difficulty,
Not to Exempt Us from Them

When a problem confronts a couple, one of two things will happen: The problem will either drive the two closer to the Lord and each other, or the problem will cause division and bitterness. The Bible assures us, however, that God is with us even in the midst of troubles. Hard times do not need to separate us from His presence, as the following passages clearly show.

Key Scriptures

ISAIAH 43:2–3: *"When you pass through the waters, I will be with you; and through the rivers, they shall not overflow you. When you walk through the fire, you shall not be burned, nor shall the flame scorch you. For I am the LORD your God, the Holy One of Israel, your Savior."*

NAHUM 1:7: *The LORD is good, a stronghold in the day of trouble; And He knows those who trust in Him.*

EPHESIANS 1:11: *In Him also we have obtained an inheritance, being predestined according to the purpose of Him who works all things according to the counsel of His will.*

ROMANS 8:28: *And we know that all things work together for good to those who love God, to those who are the called according to His purpose.*

When Susan asked the question about her little baby struggling for life in Children's Hospital, I knew that a trite answer would never satisfy her. We walked out into the hallway and talked. Tears coursed down her cheeks, and I listened. Realizing that I needed to hear the entire story (Proverbs 18:13 says, "He who answers a matter before he hears it, It is folly and shame to him"), I arranged a series of counseling sessions.

Susan eventually understood that the baby's problem was not God's punishment of her sin, nor had the devil singled her out to inflict his cruelty. She also came to a new understanding of who God really is.

THE ISSUE OF FORGIVENESS

In the process of helping Susan, I had to help her learn what it means to seek and find the forgiveness of God. She also needed to forgive her parents for the suffering she had endured because of their attitudes, and finally she had to learn to forgive herself as well for what she did in her teenage years before she became a Christian. Let's deal with those three major issues.

What Does God's Forgiveness Mean and Why Seek It?

When a relationship with another person is broken, a person's relationship with God is also affected. Harsh words produce bitterness, and anger produces sin. In dealing with the needs of people, great healing comes in recognizing, confessing, and forsaking that sin.

When people will pray with you, they begin to vent their emotions and a tremendous catharsis takes place. Tears replace anger, and the brokenness that results helps heal fractured relationships. Finding God's forgiveness is part of phase three, the restoration phase of counseling.

Key Scriptures

1 JOHN 1:9: *If we confess our sins, He is faithful and just to forgive us our sins and to cleanse us from all unrighteousness.*

PSALM 103:12–13: *As far as the east is from the west, so far has He removed our transgressions from us. As a father pities his children, so the LORD pities those who fear Him.*

ISAIAH 43:25: *"I, even I, am He who blots out your transgressions for My own sake; and I will not remember your sins."*

MICAH 7:19: *You will cast all our sins into the depths of the sea.*

Applying the Bible's Stories of Forgiveness

The Bible is full of stories of people who sinned and were forgiven. If you are counseling a friend who fears that a broken relationship is the punishment for an earlier sin, you could point out that Moses killed a man prior to God's calling (see Exodus 2:11–14). Rahab, the prostitute who befriended the spies sent out by Joshua to investigate the land of Palestine, was of the very lineage of Christ (see Matthew 1:5). David, known as a man after God's heart, was an adulterer and a party to murder (see 2 Samuel 11). Even the apostle Paul had a stained background prior to his conversion, for he caused the persecution and death of many Christians. God forgave all of them and changed their lives, just as He will forgive the friend you are counseling.

No one is beyond God's power to bring forgiveness and healing; His hand can reach every troubled heart and life. To help people understand this concept, I often quote Psalm 103:12, which says that God has removed our sins from us as far as the east from the west, and then I ask, "How far is the east from the west?" After thinking for a minute, people usually remember that the east and the west never meet. Had the psalmist said the north from the south (the North and South Poles are some 12,420 miles apart), our sins would be a measurable distance away from us.

Isaiah 44:22 mentions that our sins are blotted out as a thick cloud, something that God will never remember against us. "You mean I will never have to give an account for the abortion I once had?" a young woman asked when I shared this Scripture with her.

"Never again!" I replied.

God's forgiveness, the result of Jesus' shedding His blood and dying in our stead, means we are forgiven, brought into the family of God, the recipients of eternal life (see John 6:47). And because He has forgiven us, we must take the next step.

Forgiving Each Other

Broken relationships mean broken people, but through forgiveness we find the grace of God that mends and heals. We cannot offer each other forgiveness, however, without confronting the truth; before we forgive others, we must first let them know how they have hurt us.

Confrontation can have positive or negative effects on a fragile relationship. It can be like the scalpel in the healing hand of a surgeon—or it can be a knife that brings destruction. For it to be a positive healing force, you should observe the following:

Choose the Time, Place, and Manner of Confrontation

This gives you time to release your anger and pray about the encounter. It gives you time to think through what you want to say and what you don't want to say. Sometimes you need to get a handle on your emotions before you deal with issues. It's okay to say, "John, I'd like to talk with you about. . .after dinner this evening. That will give me time to get a handle on my feelings so I can say what I'm thinking and not say the wrong thing."[2]

Deal with the Issue; Don't Attack the Person

Saying, "Your brother is a no-good bum!" will make sparks fly. After all, your wife is related to her brother —even if he did come for a visit and stay three months, eating your food, drinking your Cokes, munching potato chips in your easy chair in front of your TV. In fact, your wife was her brother's sister long before she became your wife. So instead you might want to say, "What can we do to help your brother find a job?" That way you focus on the problem of unemployment rather than the brother's personal habits.

Express Feelings in a Nonthreatening Way

One way to do this is by using "I" messages. In other

words, if you say, "I feel that. . . ," the person listening is less likely to feel defensive than if you said, "You did [such-and-such]." When you say, "*I* have a problem and I need your help," the person whom you are confronting stops being a combatant and becomes part of the problem-solving process.

Learn to Negotiate

Another term is "compromise," but that word has a connotation we try to avoid. Life is a matter of give and take (not "I give and you take"), and harsh, unbending attitudes do not resolve conflicts. The person who refuses to yield may win the battle but lose the war.

Forgiveness means you surrender your right to hurt someone because they hurt you. It means that you extend the right to be wrong to someone else. After all, that's the very thing that God has done for you.

Remember Susan? She hadn't wronged her parents. Actually, their harsh discipline and improper understanding of God ("God's going to get you when you are bad!") was what had crippled her emotionally. However, her attitude toward them was wrong. Eventually, she came to understand that her reaction to the wrong done to her by her parents was as wrong in a different way as the injustice she had sustained. She had to be willing to forgive them for the past, so that she could go on to negotiate a new relationship with them in the present.

Most of us prefer to avoid confrontation. We also hate to go to someone and say, "I'm sorry; forgive me!" Yet Jesus said that is exactly what we need to do. Only by confronting the truth can we eventually find forgiveness. As a counselor-friend, your part is to provide the support and encouragement that will help someone face this type of painful encounter.

Key Scriptures

MATTHEW 6:14–15: *"For if you forgive men their trespasses, your heavenly Father will also forgive you. But if you do not forgive men their trespasses, neither will your Father forgive your trespasses."*

LUKE 17:3: *"Take heed to yourselves. If your brother sins against you, rebuke him; and if he repents, forgive him."*

EPHESIANS 4:32: *And be kind to one another, tenderhearted, forgiving one another, even as God in Christ forgave you.*

MATTHEW 18:15: *"Moreover if your brother sins against you, go and tell him his fault between you and him alone. If he hears you, you have gained your brother."*

Forgiving Yourself

It is often easier to seek God's forgiveness than to for-give ourselves for what we have done, especially when we feel our mistakes have harmed our children. In some cases, our failures *do* affect our children, as well as our mates. In this case, we must accept the hurtful consequences of our actions and do what we can to make amends. Once we have genuinely repented and found God's forgiveness, when we have sought and received the forgiveness of those we have hurt, then we must forgive ourselves as well.

Working through this with Susan took a period of weeks. Two passages helped her: Romans 8:14–17 and Galatians 4:4–6. Both of them describe the way God sends forth His Spirit into our hearts at con-version, adopting us into His family. The word used in the New Testament for adoption was a legal word that literally meant "the placing of a son." Human adoption illustrates the great truth of God's love for us. An infant, rejected by her biological parents or orphaned by circumstances no one could control, is accepted and loved by someone else. In the same way, God accepts us into His family.

In Bible days, when an individual was adopted by someone, he went before a judge and a legal trans-action took place. He received a new name and a new family. The past was forever obliterated, to the ex-tent that if a person had committed crimes under his old identity, he could never be held responsible for them now. In the sight of the law, the old person ceased to exist; a new one came into being.

When broken relationships are restored, our emotions are also healed, as we will discuss in the next chapter. But before we move on, I want to tell you one more thing about Susan.

That little baby with five tiny holes in her heart, then only a few days old, didn't die by age two as the doctors had predicted. Amazingly, the holes in her heart knit on their own. Her doctors didn't understand why it happened, but it happened.

Susan and I, though, have some idea why. As I counseled with her, I prayed, "Oh God, let that child live so that this mother will know that when You forgive us, You wipe the slate as clean as though we had never sinned. Help her to understand that You don't punish our children for sins that You have forgiven!"

The last time I heard from Susan, her baby had become a very normal teenager!

QUESTIONS FOR
THOUGHT AND DISCUSSION

1. Do you think most relationship problems are caused by sin? Why or why not?

2. Do you have a negative image of God or a positive one? What things have led to your image of Him? What sort of God does Christ show us? Do you think this is the same image presented by most churches?

3. Why does God want us to have healthy relationships?

4. Why are most of us uncomfortable with confrontation? What are we afraid of? How can the Bible help us to overcome our fears?

CHAPTER 8

USING THE BIBLE TO COUNSEL EMOTIONAL PROBLEMS

Time and space do not allow me to deal completely with the subject of how you help people who are struggling with emotional problems. Instead, I'll apply scriptural principles to four major emotions that are interwoven with many of the problems that bring people to you as a counselor-friend: anger, fear, worry, and depression.

Emotions are to life what pigment is to paint: They make life bright and beautiful, or dark and dreary. Indeed, without emotions life would be mechanical and lacking in intensity. But when emotions become damaged, just as when a river that overflows its banks creates destruction, something beautiful becomes ugly. When a person becomes overwhelmed by his emotions, his family, friends, and acquaintances suffer too. As a result, his own internal turmoil is even worse, and he must face it by himself, often alone and misunderstood.

First of all, though, before we go any further, I want to confront one issue: Does God really want His children to suffer emotionally? Is God pleased when we are overwhelmed with worry or fear? Is He pleased when two who once loved each other are continually torn by emotional conflict? Is He glorified in any way when people who were once productive become stressed out to the point of emotional "burnout"? The question I am asking here is not whether emotional conflict is normal or acceptable—but whether God is pleased by our succumbing to our emotions.

As always, we can turn to the Bible for the answer. In the upper room, shortly before Jesus faced Calvary, He told the disciples, "In the world you will have tribulation; but be of good cheer, I have overcome the world" (John 16:33). The word translated "tribulation" is a word that is also translated in the New Testament as oppression, affliction, or difficult circumstances.[1] All of this spells emotional pressure —or stress, as we often refer to it today.

The apostle Paul saw more than his fair share of emotional conflict. His commitment to Jesus Christ and his determination to make Christ known created conflict, just as our faith today does in some situations. The letter that we know as 2 Corinthians has been called the "heart of Paul." In this magnificent passage, Paul laid aside the doctrinal concerns that had occupied much of his previous letter, and instead, he intimately shared his heart with these struggling people, who were so immature in their own Christian experiences. Possibly, Paul wanted them to know that even he struggled with emotional issues and conflicts, but he also wanted them to know that the struggle isn't the important thing—the victory is what counts.

He wrote, "Thanks be to God who always leads us in triumph in Christ" (2 Corinthians 2:14).

Ponder these words for a moment:

From the Jews five times I received forty stripes minus one. Three times I was beaten with rods; once I was stoned; three times I was ship-wrecked; a night and a day I have been in the deep; in journeys often, in perils of waters, in perils of robbers, in perils of my own country-men, in perils of the Gentiles, in perils in the city, in perils in the wilderness, in perils in the sea, in perils among false brethren; in weari-ness and toil, in sleeplessness often, in hunger and thirst, in fastings often, in cold and nakedness—besides the other things, what comes upon me daily: my deep concern for all the churches. 2 CORINTHIANS 11:24–28

In the same letter, Paul said he was "sorrowful, yet always rejoicing; as poor, yet making many rich; as having nothing, and yet possessing all things" (2 Corinthians 6:10). What a contrast of emotions!

Whatever we face, Paul probably experienced, too. Shortly before his death, the tough old warrior wrote from prison to a young man: "God has not given us a spirit of fear, but of power and of love and of a sound mind" (2 Timothy 1:7). That sound mind principle is possible because of these things:

- A relationship with Jesus Christ deals with the fundamental issue of guilt and forgiveness.
- The Bible teaches us how to handle the disappointments and hardships that are very much part of the broken world in which we live.
- Faith eliminates the ultimate fear of death, allowing us to focus on living vibrant, meaningful, and purposeful lives.

Paul's letters echo what he experienced in life: In the world we will face trouble and pressure, but through faith in God we can overcome the emotional conflicts and pressures that are fatal to many.

Once, in San Diego, a hot-air balloon was being filled for flight. In the process, however, the balloon pulled loose from its anchorage. Some of the people holding the ropes that had anchored the balloon immediately let go. Meanwhile, others held on tightly, thinking they could hold the balloon steady. The balloon slowly lifted from the ground, and eventually some of these people could no longer hang on and plunged to their death below. A few, however, seeing what was happening, pulled themselves up the rope, hand over hand; making a loop in the rope, they rode with the balloon as it lazily drifted in the air.

Paul was like these people who managed to ride the catastrophe. He refused to give up when he was confronted with emotional issues that would have caused lesser people to "let go" and give up. "I know how to be abased," he wrote, "and I know how to abound. . .I have learned both to be full and to be hungry, both to abound and to suffer need." Then he added, "I can do all things through Christ who strengthens me" (Philippians 4:12–13).

Yeah, yeah, you may be thinking. *That's all fine and good for someone like the apostle Paul. But I'm not one of those super guys who can climb the rope and ride it out.* The point of Paul's life and teachings, though, is that the circumstances of life cannot dictate our emotional and spiritual responses. We either become overcomers or we are overcome by the circumstances.

When someone comes to you for help and you sense that your friend's mind has been poisoned with hatred and anger, you understand from the beginning that you are working with a situation that is contrary to God's will. God *does not* want us to be overcome by our emotions. That is why in this situation you can be certain that you are working in cooperation with the Spirit of God as you help your friend forsake anger and embrace forgiveness.

When you see a mother overwhelmed with irrational fear that keeps her captive within her own home, destroying her peace of mind to the point that she cannot back the family car down the driveway and take her children to school, you are dealing with a situation that is not God's will. (Remember 2 Timothy 1:7, quoted earlier in this chapter?)

When you talk with a business colleague who

has made some poor investments and is so worried about the money that he can't sleep nights and lives on a diet of double-strength Maalox and crackers, you know you are working with someone who needs the peace that comes only through Jesus Christ.

When our Christian faith becomes the framework for our emotions, our outlook will be far different from the secular mind-set. As Paul wrote, "Let this mind be in you which was also in Christ Jesus" (Philippians 2:5).

Scott Bailey, one of our volunteers at Guidelines, was injured in a sports accident when he was a teenager and spent twenty-nine days in a coma. His recovery was marked by long years of physical therapy and trips to specialists of various kinds. In spite of the physical handicap, which Scott will live with for the rest of his life, his outlook is bright, upbeat, and reflects the faith he has in his heart. When Scott was chided by an acquaintance who accused him of making his faith "a crutch," Scott replied, "Crutch, nothing! Jesus Christ has been my whole hospital!"

Christ does not guarantee that His followers will never encounter stress or conflict. But He does promise that we need not be overwhelmed by our emotional reactions to these difficulties.

Now let's examine some of the emotions you will encounter as you help others.

Already in this book we've discussed several situations that involved anger: the husband who struck his wife when she didn't like the kitchen he was remodeling; the young mother who was angry with God for allowing her baby to be born with a defective heart; the wife who was angry and hurt because of her husband's affair. The wife who has been betrayed by her husband is understandably angry, a whole different story from the husband whose temper causes him to strike his wife or children. One is the result of confidence that has been betrayed; the other occurs simply because the man's emotions are out of control. As you talk with others, you will undoubtedly encounter many other people whose anger is out of control for many different reasons.

Anger in itself is not sin. It is amoral; it can either be used for good or misused, causing a great deal of heartache. In the King James Version of the Bible, the word "anger" occurs 234 times in 228 verses; the word "angry" 44 times in 43 verses. Many of those references have to do with God's anger because of the sins of His people. Jesus was angry with the Pharisees because of their unbelief (see Mark 3:5). Obviously, He was angry when He took a whip and drove the moneychangers from the temple. There is a time and a place for anger, but when anger is demonstrated in the wrong place, at the wrong time, and in the wrong manner, it becomes sin. That is why Paul urged the Ephesians to "be angry, and do not sin" (Ephesians 4:26). One of your challenges is to help your friend handle anger, especially misdirected or unjustified anger.

Paul recognized that wrath (strong anger) often works against us, provoking us to do things we later regret (see 1 Thessalonians 5:9 and 1 Timothy 2:8). James 1:19 says we are to be "slow to wrath." After the passage where Paul urges us to be angry without sin, he says, "Do not let the sun go down on your wrath" (Ephesians 4:26).

Here are some techniques to help people work through uncontrollable or harmful anger:

- *If possible, determine the cause of the person's anger and see if anything can be done about removing its source.* This solution may require changes in lifestyle or even environment, so that people and situations that cause the anger are no longer encountered. If the source of anger can't be removed. . .

- *Encourage your friend to evaluate whether the cause of his anger is worth the emotional energy he is spending on it.* Vance Havner used to say, "Any bulldog can whip a skunk, but sometimes it just ain't worth it!"

- *Help your friend find appropriate ways of communicating feelings of anger without saying or doing things that would harm others.* For instance, help your friend talk through his anger. Expressing his anger to you, rather than the person to whom it is directed, may help to diffuse the intensity of his feelings. Or you may want to use role playing to teach your friend appropriate ways to express anger, ways that are not destructive or violent.

- *Suggest ways to relieve the stress that leads to angry outbursts.* Physical recreation or leisure activities can serve as safety valves to vent emotional pressure.

- *Help your friend realize that the indwelling presence of the Holy Spirit can tame his temper.* Prayer is the means to accomplishing this; through prayer we allow the Spirit to enter our emotions and take control.

Key Scriptures

Ephesians 4:26 (quoted previously) provides leverage for change. Ask your friend to memorize it with you. James 1:19 also gives motivation in dealing with this issue, as does 1 Thessalonians 5:9 and 1 Timothy 2:8. Make a note of these references in your Bible.

IRRATIONAL FEARS

Fear can be healthy or destructive. Fear of danger motivates a person to take steps to insure her safety; continual debilitating, enervating fear, however, shackles a person and robs the individual of peace of mind. This sort of fear does not come from God, and it must be overcome. Remember, though, that ridiculing someone's fear never helps. If you tell your friend how foolish it is to be afraid, you will only intimidate him or her and make the problem worse.

Most of our fears center around what has not happened yet but what we fear may happen; we also fear what we do not understand. Men tend to fear things that threaten their male image, such as losing their employment or the respect of their contemporaries. Women fear the loss of their physical beauty; they fear whatever robs them of their security.

Let me give you an example of an irrational fear. Your friend Joy misses Bible study for several weeks, and you drop by to see her. As you sit down for a cup of tea together, you let her know that she has been missed. At first she talks about the babysitter who couldn't take care of the children, but then she bursts into tears and says, "Oh, I might as well tell you what's really bothering me. I don't know what's gotten into me, but lately when I start to back the car out of the driveway, my hands get cold and sweaty and my heart beats like crazy. I'm scared to death that I'm going to be hit by another car. I don't know what's the matter with me. Dean says I must be losing my mind. Do you think I'm crazy?"

You answer, "No, of course not—but do you think that there may be some connection between your feelings and the automobile accident you had last year?"

"I've thought about that. I don't know."

Ridicule or criticism won't work; instead, encourage Joy to take one small step toward letting go of her irrational fear. You might persuade her to ride with you to the post office a block away. . .and then perhaps she will be able to drive you both to your kids' school a mile away. Care enough to go with her as she continues to make a few small trips. If she cannot bring herself to drive herself anywhere yet, be accepting and supportive. Allow her to accept the reality of her fear and then encourage her not to allow her fear to keep her from living her life. Encourage her to take the bus or find a ride with another person.

Shortly after Darlene and I married, I learned that she had acrophobia (fear of heights). We had taken the elevator up to the Eiffel Tower in Paris and to save a little money, we'd decided to walk down. We had only gone a short ways down the stairs through the tower's exterior when she froze, and I discovered that heights really frighten her.

Three years ago, as we were skiing, she stopped on a slope, petrified of coming down. I had skied a few hundred yards further and kept waiting for her to follow. About then a ski patrol on a skimobile came by. I stopped him and asked him to go up and give her a ride down.

"Honey, it's okay; you don't have to ski. It's all right," I told her. Instead of downhill skiing, we've discovered the joy of cross-country skiing, something that she enjoys far more.

Nothing outside God's will can happen to the child of God who is living according to His purposes. That knowledge removes the feeling of being victimized by circumstances. Jack Morris, the psychotherapist I mentioned earlier, uses Psalm 23 with patients who are struggling with fear, asking them to memorize the psalm and quote it audibly several times a day. "Yea, though I walk through the valley of the shadow of death, I will fear no evil; for You are with me"(verse 4).

Using the promises in Psalm 23, you can help people cope with circumstances that could otherwise produce devastating fear. Once they understand that safety is not "the absence of danger" but "the promise of the Lord's protection," they can live above fear. Fear will no longer destroy their peace of mind.

Key Scriptures

2 TIMOTHY 1:7: *For God has not given us a spirit of fear, but of power and of love and of a sound mind.*

PSALM 23:4: *Yea, though I walk through the*

valley of the shadow of death, I will fear no evil; for You are with me; Your rod and Your staff, they comfort me.

PERVASIVE WORRY

No matter how many of us indulge in the practice, worry is sin. No one can worry and trust God at the same time; you have to help your friend see this truth if you are to help him overcome what has been described as "the acceptable sin of the saints." Some people, because of their nature and emotional make-up, are more prone to worry than others are, yet anxiety or worry is not justifiable merely because it "comes naturally."

When a friend struggling with this problem asks you, "What do you think I should do about it?" you need to work through several issues. First, what is the actual cause of concern or worry? Has your friend determined whether or not the issue is valid? For example, if the woman in your Bible study who asks you to pray with her about "her cancer" has never gone to the doctor for an examination, the first step is to convince her that she needs a proper medical diagnosis.

Elderly people are often quite certain they will run out of money before they die (no matter how much money they have). Getting that person to consult with a financial planner or a bank who can help with investments may allay their concern. Or the person who is worried about personal finances may eliminate that concern by having a budget and learning to stay within it.

Your part as a counselor-friend may be to provide the emotional support to insure that action is taken. You can also suggest that your friend read *Worry-Free Living* by Dr. Frank Minirth, Dr. Paul Meier, and Don Hawkins.

Last, has the person who is worried made the matter a definite, concerned issue for prayer? Committing yourself to the keeping of a sovereign God, believing that He is in control of your life, eliminates worry. You can then turn out the light and say, "God, you take the night shift; no need for both of us to stay awake. I'm going to sleep!" Prayer works!

Key Scripture

PHILIPPIANS 4:6–7: *Be anxious for nothing, but in everything by prayer and supplication, with thanksgiving, let your requests be made known to God; and the peace of God, which surpasses all understanding, will guard your hearts and minds through Christ Jesus.* (The truth of this passage comes through clearly in The Living Bible paraphrase, which says, *Don't worry about anything; instead, pray about everything.*)

EMOTIONAL DEPRESSION

In phase one of the counseling process, you are striving to understand what the problem really is and what is causing it. When your friend comes to you depressed, your first task is to help her evaluate the cause of her depression.

Among the causes of depression, look for the following:

- suppressed anger
- hopelessness
- secret habits or problems
- physical problems requiring the care of a doctor

As you talk with a friend, you begin to determine whether his or her sadness is the result of a specific cause (say, because an aerospace engineer, age forty-seven, is laid off and now is overly qualified for a menial position, and can't find employment in his field of expertise) or if your friend is struggling with a chronic depression which just doesn't go away. Some of the symptoms of depression are lethargy, indifference to responsibilities, neglected appearance, and emotional flatness.

In situations involving chronic fatigue, I always recommend that the friend go for a complete physical, with care given to blood sugar and composition. If no physical reason for depression becomes evident, your friend needs the help of a professional. At times depression can be relieved by a change of diet, a program of physical exercise under a physician's supervision, or even a low dose of medication to stabilize a chemical imbalance in the body.

While depression itself is not hereditary, the predisposition to certain personality types that are more susceptible to depression or discouragement can be inherited. That's one reason you should never make a depressed person feel guilty for her feelings. Telling a depressed individual to "snap out of it" because God doesn't want her depressed only drives her deeper into depression. However, you should assure the person that God cares and that He will never leave or forsake His child (see Key Scriptures on page 171). When your friend understands that he or she has been forgiven and is God's child, that knowledge will help overcome depression.

Diagnose the problem, but minister to the whole person, including the physical, the emotional, and the spiritual.

The Physical Body and Depression

When people tell me about depression, I always ask, "What kind of physical exercise do you get?" Invariably, the person gets none—or else he walks around the block thinking, "What a workout!" As a result of counseling people, I have become convinced that physical exertion is one of the best antidotes to depression available today. If I have any question about a person's physical condition, however, I send him to a doctor to find out how much exercise he can safely handle. I then recommend that he start walking (build up to a brisk walk of three to five miles at least three times weekly) or get some other exercise that will increase the heartbeat and the rate of respiration.

Depression and Your Spiritual Life

In striving to isolate the reason for depression, you may discover that your friend is living with something that he or she knows is wrong. Gordon MacDonald refers to this type of person as a "secret carrier," someone who may be struggling with a sin such as an immoral relationship, an addiction to pornography, or a financial shenanigan that your friend knows is wrong. Bringing that problem to light, dealing with it through repentance, confession, and restitution (when necessary) will eliminate depression.

The person who is depressed for spiritual reasons almost always feels that God is distant and that prayer doesn't work. Even John the Baptist, languishing in dark Machaerus Prison, probably succumbed to doubt and eventual depression, wondering whether or not Jesus was really the Christ. Depressed people usually doubt truths that they really know are valid (just as John did). In their hearts they know that God has not singled them out as victims of attack, yet they feel isolated and lonely.

When a friend of mine had a heart attack, he lay in the hospital thinking of the speaking engagements that would have to be canceled, the writing deadlines that would not be met, and how his meager finances would be stretched by the illness. As he cried out, "Why me, Lord?" he seemed to hear the echo return, "Why not you?" Isaiah 43:2 reminds us that we will face the valley, the fire, and the flood—but the promise that we must claim by faith is that He walks with us.

Key Scriptures

MATTHEW 28:20: *"Lo, I am with you always, even to the end of the age."*

HEBREWS 13:5–6: *"I will never leave you nor forsake you." So we may boldly say: "The Lord is my helper; I will not fear. What can man do to me?"*

Depression and Your Emotional Life

Recognizing that the spiritual cannot be separated from the emotional, we need to point out that the person who is depressed not only doubts spiritual truths, but he likewise finds it difficult to accept other valid realities. ("My wife really doesn't love me, or else she would understand how I feel!") Here you can help your friend understand that love is a commitment, and that his wife is standing by the commitment that was made long ago.

A person's emotions are controlled by the will, and the decision to hold on to reality goes a long way toward breaking through depression (see *Happiness Is a Choice* by Dr. Frank Minirth and Dr. Paul Meier[2]). In our Guidelines publication *Depression Stoppers*,[3] I point out that praise is a matter of the will. It is one of the tools that God has given us to fight the emotional "blahs" of depression. Your friend needs to focus on the goodness of God, His character and faithfulness, and begin to recount the various ways God still smiles upon him. He needs to say, "Lord, I know You are sovereign and in control of the universe. I also believe that You are greater than my depression, and I thank You for what You have done for me and for what You are going to do." As he makes this prayer, his depression will begin to lift. Happiness is a choice!

QUESTIONS FOR THOUGHT AND DISCUSSION

1. Can you explain the difference between experiencing emotional conflict—and being overwhelmed by our emotions?

2. Have you ever felt guilty for experiencing a negative emotion? What do you think the apostle Paul would say? (See 2 Corinthians 2:14.)

3. Why is worry a sin?

4. In what way is happiness a choice?

CHAPTER 9

USING THE BIBLE TO COUNSEL ADDICTIVE BEHAVIOR

As we approach the subject of addictive behavior, you may be tempted to throw up your hands and say, "Whoa, this is too much for me. Someone who is addicted to something needs a professional!" Clearly, many times you would be right—but I'll give you guidelines that will help you know when to steer someone toward professional help.

In some cases, though, people don't have money for treatment. They don't understand that many professional groups, including the majority of Christian counseling services, have sliding scales that make it possible for almost anyone to get help. Also, often people are unwilling to place themselves under the care of a professional whom they do not know or trust. They will, however, turn to a friend and ask for help. Sometimes the parents or the mate of someone who is hurting will be the one who asks, "What do you think I should do?" You need to be prepared to answer.

Addictive behavior is a pattern of activity that demonstrates emotional or physical dependence on something or someone. It may be a physical dependency, as in substance abuse (alcohol and drugs). In other cases, the addictive behavior is an emotional dependency or attachment.

Please understand that my treatment of each subject in this chapter is rather superficial. My goal is merely to point out how to identify the addictive problem so that you can help your friend see the implications of what he or she is doing. Your friend will also need to see the implications of ignoring the issue. Along with this, I want to make you acquainted with Scripture passages that will help release the power of the Holy Spirit. God's Spirit is the greatest force in all the world when it comes to changing behavior patterns.

DEFINING YOUR LIMITATIONS AS A COUNSELOR-FRIEND

When you encounter addictive behavior, you are always confronted with the question, "Can I help?" The answer to that question depends on whether or not the person who is hurting will allow you to help.

If the person does want your help, the questions that follow will give you guidelines for determining whether you personally should undertake the counseling task—or whether you should make a referral and then support your friend as he follows through with treatment.

How Will the Individual
Respond to Confrontation?

If the person with the problem is the one who has come to you and asked, "What do you think I should do?" the confrontation issue is not difficult. It is more complex, however, when a mother says, "I was cleaning my son's room this morning and I found an envelope of white powder I think is cocaine. My son says it isn't his. He says it belonged to the boy who spent the night over the weekend. But I don't believe him. My husband and I think he's a user." In that case, the only way for you to become involved is through confrontation.

Confrontation makes most of us uncomfortable, but it is absolutely necessary if we want to help someone with an addiction. Often described as "tough love," this kind of confrontation means that a family is willing to say, "Look, you've got a problem. You know it, and we do, too; but we love you so much that we insist you get help. We're going to stand with you, but this cannot go on. You've got to have help." As a friend, you, too, can confront people with the same loving firmness. If you are engaged in lay counseling, the issues of wrongdoing and poor choices must also be confronted.

Is the Person Willing to Face
the Consequences of His or Her Actions?

In phase two of the counseling process, you strive to help your friend see the options that are available and the ultimate consequences of her choices. As long as a person refuses to acknowledge there *is* a problem, the individual hasn't faced the consequences of his or her actions. Thus, until your friend acknowledges that substance abuse or continued addictive behavior is damaging or destroying family relations, the abuse will continue and increase in severity.

Does the Person Have the Desire to Change?

Most people who ask for help with some kind of addictive behavior really *want* help. One of the beautiful things about counseling in the Spirit's power is that God will help anyone who acknowledges his need and turns to the Lord. You are like a midwife whose efforts will be accompanied by pain and travail. When a person comes to you primarily because someone else wants him to come, however, to get the "monkey off his back," you can do very little. When I find myself in this situation, I often say, "Look, I don't think you are ready for us to work together in this problem. I want you to know that I care and I'm available, and when you are ready to work with me, I'm ready to help."

Will the Person Be
Completely Honest with Me?

My experience has always been that a person's honesty has a direct relationship to my ability to help him or her. Deception and dishonesty indicate that the person hasn't yet reached the point where he or she is truly willing to accept help. When people lie to me, I tell them that I can't help them. I'll still be their friend, but there is no point in either of us wasting time discussing lies.

Is the Person Willing to be Accountable?

Accountability means a person is willing to show up punctually for appointments; it also means he can accept the responsibility for his actions. Also, when someone comes to you for help, and at the same time he also goes to one or two other people for help, I would recommend that you refer the person to one of the other counselors. Or you might ask that only the two of you work together until you have had a chance to see what God is going to do. The other counselors' goals may be exactly the same as yours, but the manner in which they go about reaching those goals may be at cross-purposes with what you are trying to accomplish. If your friend is serious about getting help for his problem, he will be willing to commit to working through it with one person, rather than jumping from one approach to another.

Is the Person Comfortable Working with Me?

Is your friend sincerely willing to accept the counsel and direction you give? The accountability that we've already discussed means acknowledging some embarrassing or distasteful things. These may be hard for your friend to admit within the context of your friendship. Sometimes when a person is close to you and your family, you may want to refer your hurting friend to a professional for help.

You probably won't get an unqualified and enthusiastic "Yes!" answer to all of these six questions. And as the counseling process flows, sometimes you may think you are making little headway. However, as long as you see a person is striving to work with you, you can be successful in helping your friend.

When you are dispensing lay counseling, particularly to someone who is addicted, there is always a good chance that the person you are trying to counsel will ignore your advice and make a choice that you believe is a poor one. What happens to your friendship then?

Your friend will probably avoid you. He or she will feel awkward whenever you run into each other.

But you need to let your friend know that no matter what happens, you still love him or her and want to be a friend. Your love and friendship are not dependent on your friend's behavior; they are unconditional.

Jesus had that kind of love for His disciples. The week prior to His death on Calvary, He instructed the disciples to love each other, as He loved them (see John 13:34–35)—and His love separated acceptance from behavior. At times, He reached out to people in love and concern, and they responded by loving Him in return. At other times, they turned and walked away, rejecting His love. But His love for them was not diminished by their rejection or personal failures.

As a counselor, you cannot force your friend to follow your advice, no matter how right you may be. But you can continue to love your friend the way Jesus loved those to whom He ministered.

ALCOHOL ABUSE

While the Bible does not teach abstinence when it comes to the use of alcoholic beverages, it does teach moderation. The wine of the first century was a beverage with approximately one-third the alcoholic content of wine today. It also was used as an antiseptic and a medicine. Paul instructed Timothy: "No longer drink only water, but use a little wine for your stomach's sake and your frequent infirmities" (1 Timothy 5:23). In the story of the Good Samaritan (see Luke

10:30–37), the Samaritan poured oil and wine into the wounds of the injured man.

Drunkenness or alcoholic dependency is clearly forbidden by Scripture. Romans 13:13 says, "Let us walk properly, as in the day, not in revelry and drunkenness." Drunkenness is also singled out as one of the manifestations of the flesh in Galatians 5:21.

Most of the people who struggle with alcoholism are generally aware that the Bible condemns their problem; they just don't know what to do about it. Until they accept the fact that they have a problem with alcohol, you won't be effective as a counselor-helper. At Alcoholics Anonymous, people begin their testimony with the words, "I am an alcoholic." Recognizing their problem opens the door for solutions. Often your best contribution may be to help your friend admit his problem—and then support him as he begins treatment in a dependency center or in Alcoholics Anonymous.

The motivation to overcome any dependency must be stronger than the force of the addiction. For a child of God, an understanding that his or her body is the temple of the Holy Spirit of God (see Romans 12:1–2 and 1 Corinthians 6:19) can be a great motive for change. As you work with your friend, try to remember that the Holy Spirit is the agent of behavioral change, and that the individual is responsible and can change. As you pray with your friend, expect change. Don't be satisfied until change takes place.

Some people are delivered instantaneously from a dependency on alcohol, but most alcoholics need help and encouragement over a long period of time. Family support as well as your support as a counselor-friend is vital. If you don't have the time or the emotional energy to offer this type of long-term involvement, you would be wise to make a referral to an alcohol abuse support group such as Overcomers Outreach, a church-related group. The number of these groups is growing, and you should be able to find one by consulting your yellow pages or your pastor.

Key Scriptures

EPHESIANS 5:18: *Do not be drunk with wine, in which is dissipation; but be filled with the Spirit.*

ROMANS 14:21: *It is good neither to eat meat nor drink wine nor do anything by which your brother stumbles or is offended or is made weak.*

DRUG ABUSE

In our generation, drug abuse has escalated in an unprecedented fashion. No one set of circumstances accounts for the use of drugs today, but probably the greatest factor in drug abuse is peer pressure. Among young adults cocaine and crack (free-based cocaine, sold in ready-to-smoke form) have become the drugs of choice. (See Ross Campbell, *Your Child and Drugs,* published by Scripture Press.)

Your job as a counselor-friend includes determining whether your friend has been involved in recreational drug abuse (occasional use) or if he has developed an actual drug dependency. A person who is truly chemically addicted will stop at nothing to support the craving that his body has for drugs. This leads to other immoral behaviors that only compound the severity of the problem.

Drug dependency goes far beyond cocaine. A growing number of people are dependent on amphetamines and weight control medication. Whether it is cocaine or caffeine (from tea, coffee, or carbonated beverages), a person is addicted when he feels physical discomfort ("I'll get a headache without my coffee.") because of its absence.

Many people who dabble in drugs could have been saved tremendous heartache if someone had picked up on their problem early enough and cared enough to confront them. Once a person is addicted to the point that he or she is physically affected, you will need to encourage your friend to get professional help, perhaps even a drug rehabilitation program where there is supervised help on a twenty-four-hour basis.

Many people struggling with addictions can successfully be helped by counselor-friends who care enough to ride out the storm. Several suggestions may be helpful as you work through the counseling process:

- *Remember, from a Christian's perspective, dependence on drugs is a matter of choice.* Your friend became addicted as the result of choices he made. (You are unlikely to counsel someone who became addicted to a substance because someone forced drugs on him.) Likewise, freedom from addiction can come through the decision to resist and live a drug-free life. If drug addiction is harmful (and it is), then it is also sin before God and should be dealt with as such.

- *Complete and absolute dependence upon the Lord is necessary for deliverance.* The person who kicks a drug habit "cold turkey" without help is a rare and strong individual; most need help, and that's where you come into the picture as a counselor-friend. The Lord can use you to demonstrate His constant love and support.

- *Help your friend develop independence from her peer group.* This is probably one of your most important functions. Slogans like "Just say no!" are well and good, but when a person's best friends urge him or her to say "Yes!" slogans are meaningless. Help restructure the environment by offering the support necessary to change the peer group. You will need to steer your friend toward a church or support group where he or she can hear people say, "Man, I can relate to your problem. That's where I was two years ago, but God gave me deliverance and now I'm clean." A new peer group, one that offers support rather than pressure, can reverse drug use from participation to restraint.

• *Use the power of prayer as you work with a person* (more about this in the chapter to follow).

Key Scriptures

1 CORINTHIANS 6:19–20: *Do you not know that your body is the temple of the Holy Spirit who is in you, whom you have from God, and you are not your own? For you were bought at a price; therefore glorify God in your body and in your spirit, which are God's.* (These five powerful words are motives for change: "You are not your own." Then to whom do you belong? To Jesus Christ.)

1 PETER 1:18–19: *Knowing that you were not redeemed with corruptible things, like silver or gold. . .but with the precious blood of Christ. . .* (Our lives have been paid for by Christ's precious blood. That makes them infinitely valuable—not something to be thrown away in drug addiction.)

SEXUAL ADDICTION

Webster's New Collegiate Dictionary defines the verb "addict" as "to devote or surrender (oneself) to something habitually or obsessively."[1] In a sexual addiction, the person is either obsessed by unhealthy sexual thoughts or he devotes himself to infidelity and promiscuity.

Obsessive Sexual Relations

I am not talking here about someone who wants to have frequent sexual relations in marriage, nor am I referring to the manner in which people find sexual fulfillment with their mates. Neither am I talking about the teenager who has a perfectly normal curiosity about his sexual functions. What I am describing is the person whose sexual appetites have become inflamed to the point that they are unhealthy; this person is as obsessed with sex as the addict is with cocaine.

We live in a sex-addicted culture, according to Pitirim Sorokin, a Harvard University sociologist who made these charges in the early 1970s. Since then, our culture has continued to be so permeated with sex that it oozes from the pores of our national life. Sexually explicit material that would never have been allowed a few decades ago is commonplace on American television and in the theater. The video-cassette recorder has moved the X-rated movie from the theater to the home, and with today's rating standards, R-rated movies are almost as sexually explicit as X-rated films of earlier times. The Internet offers even more temptations for those obsessed with sex—while making it even easier to bring pornography into the home. As exposure breeds familiarity, millions of people who a few years ago would have strongly objected to the sex-saturation of our culture have gradually tolerated it and even embraced it.

Constant exposure to sex does one of two things: It creates either a blasé indifference or an obsession to the degree that one's perspective becomes totally distorted. Sexual addiction is a perversion of a normal appetite whose fulfillment in marriage has the blessing of God. The person who is sexually obsessed has an unsatisfied craving that is unhealthy and twisted. What normally would have satisfied no longer is sufficient. Sexual appetites remain unfulfilled.

How does this happen? Sometimes the person is looking for a missing part of his or her life: an authentic, valid relationship with someone. Looking for intimacy and companionship, the person goes from one relationship to another, driven by a desire that confuses sex with love. The person suffering from sexual obsession may be the woman who was never held and loved by her father (or her husband), and thus she confuses sexual expression with loving relationships. Other times, the man who did not relate well to women in his youth now finds a perverse satisfaction in pornography, which doesn't talk back or challenge his masculine ego. Having become addicted to pornography, he gradually turns to unsatisfying, unfulfilling sexual encounters.

How do you help a person overcome this obsession? Begin by finding out what's being fed into his mind. Ask him to tell you the names and ratings of the last five movies he has seen. If you find that pornography is a prominent part of his sexual life, ask him how long he has used it. Then help him see that sexual expression is no substitute for meaningful relationships (more about this in the section under promiscuity).

As you help your friend see himself as God sees him, you will need to label this problem sin and deal with it on that basis. Scripture says, "He who covers his sins will not prosper, But whoever confesses and forsakes them will have mercy" (Proverbs 28:13).

Replace negative sexual input with the powerful cleansing of the Word. In 2 Peter 1:4, Peter talks about escaping the corruption and lust of the world through the great promises of God's Word. Long ago the psalmist asked the question, "How can a young man cleanse his way?" and answered, "By taking heed according to Your word" (Psalm 119:9). Quoting and memorizing Scripture reprograms many of the lustful images that have become mental habits.

Insist on accountability as you work with your friend. This includes honesty, openness, and willingness to change. Be prepared for the process to take some time.

Key Scriptures

1 CORINTHIANS 3:16–17: *Do you not know that you are the temple of God and that the Spirit of God dwells in you? If anyone defiles the temple of God, God will destroy him. For the temple of God is holy, which temple you are.*

2 PETER 1:3–4: *His divine power has given to us. . .great and precious promises, that through these you may be partakers of the divine nature, having escaped the corruption that is in the world through lust.*

Promiscuity

For every married couple today, there is one single adult. Many of them fall into the ranks of the formerly married, individuals who at one time carried on normal sexual relations with a long-term partner but because of death or divorce find themselves single again. For the formerly married, sex was a very ordinary part of their relationship. It represented intimacy, the expression of love, and the emotional and physical release that accompanies orgasm.

For the formerly married, returning to celibacy is seldom easy. Loneliness and isolation often create situations that cause a person to set aside biblical values for the warmth of another human body. Casual sex has become relatively common for singles that nonetheless consider themselves to be "born again."

Of course, promiscuity is not solely the problem of the formerly married. Sexual temptations confront the teenager and the young adult eager for acceptance. Recent studies indicate that at least sixty percent of teenage girls participate in their first experience because of peer pressure.

The promiscuous person who goes from sexual partner to partner is an insecure individual, desperately seeking love and acceptance among partners whose commitment lasts only for a night. This person's emotional needs can be met only within the context of marriage.

In her book *Being a Woman,* Dr. Toni Grant, a popular psychologist, says:

> Many contemporary women with whom I speak have lots of ideas about sexuality and relationship but no standards, by which they live and share their bodies. I am constantly getting calls from women who don't know how to say no, who don't even have the language for setting standards of any sort, who are desperately afraid that if they do say no, they will lose the men in their lives.[2]

Casual sex is sex without commitment (and apart from marriage there is no lasting commitment).

Today, scores of men and women seeking satisfaction confuse sexual experience with emotional commitment. In relationships outside the commitment of marriage, the woman is often the greater loser. To her, sex is usually not merely a physical response but an emotional commitment that may not be reciprocated. She also runs the risk of dealing with the consequences of an unwanted pregnancy. Sex outside of marriage makes her emotionally and physically (in many cases, even financially) vulnerable. As Toni Grant put it, "Any way you slice it, the woman in an uncommitted sexual relationship is between a rock and a hard place. . . . Uncommitted sex has not worked very well for women."[3]

Contrary to modern thinking, however, God expects of singles the same that He expects of married couples: sexual purity. That means abstinence before marriage and commitment to one individual, your mate, in marriage. While casual sex may be the norm and have a measure of acceptance in our culture, it is wrong in the sight of God.

Key Scriptures

1 THESSALONIANS 4:3–5: *For this is the will of God. . .that you should abstain from sexual immorality; that each of you should know how to possess his own vessel (his body) in sanctification and honor, not in passion of lust, like the Gentiles who do not know God.* (In this passage, there is no ambiguity and no hedging.)

Writing to Timothy, Paul instructed the widowed young women to marry again and assume the responsibilities of a wife and mother, thereby avoiding sexual temptation (see 1 Timothy 5:11–16).

> ROMANS 12:1–2: *Present your bodies a living sacrifice, holy, acceptable to God, which is your reasonable service. And do not be conformed to this world, but be transformed by the renewing of your mind, that you may prove what is that good and acceptable and perfect will of God.* (Phillips paraphrases the words "do not be conformed to this world" as "Don't let the world around you squeeze you into its own mould.")

Infidelity in Marriage

Unfaithfulness in marriage usually ends in divorce, but it doesn't have to. Although mentioned in Scripture as valid grounds for divorce (Matthew 5:31–32; 19:4–9), unfaithfulness can be forgiven. Restoration and healing can take place. That's your goal as a counselor-friend.

When a relationship is affected by an affair, both husband and wife feel guilty. The offending party feels guilty because she (or he) knows she (or he) has sinned before God and broken the promises made at the marriage altar. The offended party also has a sense of guilt because he (or she) thinks, "If I had met her (or his) needs as I should have, if only I had kept myself as attractive as the other man (or the other woman), my wife (husband) would not have strayed!"

As you deal with this issue, try to determine if the offended party actually did contribute to the mate's failure by not meeting the needs of the one who strayed. This does not remove the responsibility from the unfaithful spouse, but it does help the offended partner accept responsibility for his part in the marriage breakdown. This may help to dispel some of the anger and hurt.

Ask a group of people, "How many does it take for a marriage to fail?" and the majority of people will respond, "Two!" At times, though, the failure of one person to meet the needs of the other is not the issue at all. The fact is that when only one person in a marriage says, "I don't want to be married to you anymore; I want my freedom," a marriage is finished. The other person cannot force the marriage to continue.

In some cases, husbands and wives may deeply love their mates; they may not feel that their mates have let them down in any way. Confronted with sexual opportunity, however, they gave into temptation. Afterward, they deeply regret what took place. This type of situation offers the greatest opportunity for forgiveness and healing.

In chapter 7, we dealt with the issue of forgiveness. Forgiveness is seldom easy, especially when the deepest of all relationships is violated, but healing *can* take place. Just as a broken bone can heal stronger than before the accident took place, a restored marriage can make a relationship deeper and more treasured because of the crisis that has been weathered.

Key Scriptures

EXODUS 20:14: *"You shall not commit adultery."* (This commandment is so important to God, that He made it one of the Ten Commandments that He gave to Moses.)

TITUS 1:6 (NIV): *An elder must be blameless, the husband of but one wife.* (This standard is not for church leaders only. God wants us to have monogamous sexual relationships.)

EPHESIANS 5:33 (NIV): *Each one of you also must love his wife as he loves himself, and the wife must respect her husband.* (This is what God wants for our marriages. In a relationship of mutual respect, where both mates love each other as much as they love themselves, there is no room for infidelity.)

Homosexuality

The traditional Judeo-Christian position is that homosexuality is one of the sexual practices condemned by God. Paul includes this lifestyle when he catalogs the former failures of the Corinthians in 1 Corinthians 6:9–10.

When you counsel individuals who practice homosexuality, remember that sexual preference is a choice, an act of the will, not a genetic predilection a person cannot control. At this writing, there is absolutely no scientific evidence for the position that an individual has been "trapped" by his genetic code. Genetics do not relieve him of his responsibility in the sight of God. For God to condemn someone for a practice he could not help would be unjust, but the fact is, homosexuality is but one of many practices God can forgive—and with His forgiveness comes His enabling power to change, something that the church is often strangely silent about proclaiming.

Always be cautious about labeling people. One or two homosexual encounters do not make someone a homosexual any more than one or two drinks make someone an alcoholic. Consistent homosexual practice, however, does result in that person being a homosexual.

My experience has been that individuals who come for counseling with this problem fall into two categories: those who want acceptance for their lifestyle and those who realize their lives are displeasing to God and want to change. We have every reason to believe that the Holy Spirit will bring deliverance to this second group. While it is difficult to reorient sexual preferences, it is not impossible, any more than it is impossible for an individual who has been delivered from alcoholism to resist when she encounters alcohol.

In counseling with homosexuals, remember that God loves the individual; it is the sin that He condemns. All too often, we condemn the person along with her sin. Strive to let your friend know that you love and accept her as a human being.

Key Scriptures

LEVITICUS 18:22: *You shall not lie with a male as with a woman. It is an abomination.* (See also Leviticus 20:13.)

1 CORINTHIANS 6:9, 11: *Homosexuals. . . And such were some of you. But you were washed, but you were sanctified, but you were justified in the name of the Lord Jesus and by the Spirit of our God.*

ROMANS 1:26–27: *For this reason God gave them up to vile passions. For even their women exchanged the natural use for what is against nature. Likewise also the men, leaving the natural use of the woman, burned in their lust for one another, men with men committing what is shameful, and receiving in themselves the penalty of their error which was due.*

COMPULSIVE EATING DISORDERS

Our English word *bulimia* is a transliteration of the Greek word that means "greater hunger." It is an eating disorder that involves gorging on food, followed by self-induced vomiting or purging. Its opposite is anorexia, self-induced starvation. Both are serious disorders.

The possibility of your helping when your friend struggles with an eating disorder depends on you following the guidelines that began this chapter. As with other addictions, your greatest contribution may be to help your friend recognize the seriousness of the problem and then guide and support her to seek professional help.

When emotional needs are met, we act in a responsible manner, but when needs are not met, a spectrum of irresponsible activities follow that may include eating disorders. Admitting their problem is one of the most difficult things for people struggling with this issue. Usually these people try to hide the problem, not wanting family or friends to know what is happening.

Take, for example, the situation described by Dori, who wrote the following to me when she discovered that her roommate, Pat, was bulimic:

Right now I am just sick to my stomach; I am so upset. The problem is Pat (my roommate). I guess I had no idea how messed up that girl is

*until the last few weeks. I have noticed that
she always disappears after meals, but I
thought it was only to get out of the dishes. She
has been doing this for a long time because [her
last year's roommate] discovered it when she
was living with her.*

*I am crushed. I deplore what Pat is inside,
and yet I am so sad and broken-hearted for
her, I can't even explain it. The thing that I
feel the very worst about is that I have lost all
respect for her as a person; she is disgusting, or
rather what she is doing is disgusting.*

Dori told me later that Pat's dad wanted a boy when
she was born; he always felt that "Patricia" should
have been "Patrick." As she grew up, her dad never
expressed as much affection for her as he did for the
other children. Money? He had plenty of it and saw
that she attended the best boarding schools and had
nice clothes and a sports car. "I know her problem was
really the result of her relationship with her dad,"
Dori said as she recounted the year she lived with Pat.

Dori was able to separate her feelings for Pat
from her revulsion for Pat's problem and remained
her friend. On the other hand, Pat never admitted
the problem and continued with the pattern into her
adult life.

Eating disorders can be serious addictive problems, equally as life-threatening as drug and alcohol
addiction, and they cannot be treated lightly. While

you may feel the problem is more serious than you can handle, you could be the link between disaster and life through your friendship, warmth, compassion, and caring. You do make a difference.

Key Scriptures

Again, Romans 12:1–2 reminds us that our bodies are to be "a living sacrifice, holy, acceptable to God."

1 Corinthians 3:16–17 says our bodies are temples of the Holy Spirit and that the Spirit of God literally indwells our bodies, giving us a motive for health.

Now, let's go on to our final chapter as I share some guidelines that will help you succeed in counseling friends.

QUESTIONS FOR
THOUGHT AND DISCUSSION

1. Why is unconditional acceptance so important to lay counseling?

2. Why do you think Dr. Sala included promiscuity, infidelity, and homosexuality under the heading of sexual addiction?

3. Do you think there is any connection between addiction and what the Bible refers to as idolatry? Why or why not?

CHAPTER 10

SUCCESSFUL COUNSELING

What makes counseling successful? For me, success means helping a person find the will of God for his life, providing the support necessary for him to move toward God's will, and then seeing him grow in his relationship with Christ. In the process, something of my life, my emotions, my intellect, my time, and my energies are invested in that person.

In my possession is a set of gold cuff links with a monogram on one link and a watch on the other. I suppose that I have worn them no more than a dozen times in my life, but I would hate to lose them —not because of their value, but because they were a gift, a token of a victory God wrought in the life of a man who had maintained a homosexual lifestyle for most of his adult life.

In San Francisco, listening to my radio program, he concluded that I could help him and called for an appointment. Then he flew more than four hundred miles each way once a week for counseling. Through the same counseling process that I have described in this book, that man came to a saving knowledge of Jesus Christ, and eventually he learned that God had a different plan for his life. The break with his former lifestyle was not an easy one, but he made it. Habits and practices that have taken years to establish are not eliminated in a matter of a few weeks. But they can be broken. This man ultimately found God's grace to reorient his lifestyle.

Success in lay counseling means seeing individuals whose lives were headed in the wrong direction make changes that give them a new hope and a new future. It means watching children grow up in a home that would have been destroyed had not God used you in some way to help a friend realize how foolish she would have been to throw away a marriage in exchange for the thrill of a make-believe, illicit relationship. It means watching individuals who could not function without the support of drugs stabilize their emotions, grow emotionally and spiritually, and relate to life in a way they never have before. Successful counseling means helping individuals rise to their full, God-given potential—not because you are so bright or clever, but because you learned the importance of letting the Holy Spirit work through you, allowing Christ to act in the life of your friend.

Yes, I freely admit that I don't win every round. Sometimes I walk away from a situation feeling that I have failed, thinking to myself, *Did I miss something? Was there anything else I should have done to make a difference?* Some things we must learn by experience, and every person who becomes proficient in lay counseling will have learned from past mistakes. In the end, though, no matter how skilled at counseling we become, we cannot force people to change.

As I look back over three decades of counseling and training others to help people, I recognize that successful counseling is the interaction of God's Holy Spirit in both my life and the life of the person who has come to me for help. God has used me as a catalyst for change, a channel for His Spirit.

Keeping in mind that God is the only One who can do miracles, let me give you four tips that will help you be a successful counselor.

SUCCESSFUL COUNSELING IS THE RESULT OF PERSEVERING UNTIL A RELATIONSHIP HAS STABILIZED

When my son Steve was in the final year of his college program, he spent a summer in Northern Luzon in the Philippines, working among a tribal group. His area of training was in biomedical engineering, and he wanted some "hands-on" medical experience in cooperation with a medical team. Aside from his communication difficulties (he didn't know the language), his greatest frustration was seeing someone who was very ill begin to take the medication he prescribed and then quit because she was feeling better, leading to a far more serious attack of the disease, simply because she didn't finish the round of antibiotics Steve had given her.

Ending counseling too soon does the same thing. The process of restoration may take time, and we should not walk away before the entire process is complete. No progress takes place in a straight line; people will make improvement, fail, try again, and fail again. Only when they stop trying altogether do they quickly begin to slide downhill in the counseling process.

How do you handle failure? In just the same way you help a child who is learning to walk: You help your friend get back on his feet, get him walking again, and gradually turn him loose. When I help a friend gain strength and maturity to overcome persistent failures, I take the person through this process each time he fails. These are the questions I ask him:

WHAT HAPPENED?

WHAT WAS YOUR RESPONSE?

WHAT SHOULD HAVE BEEN YOUR RESPONSE?

HOW CAN YOU RECTIFY THE PROBLEM NOW?

For example, listen to the following scenario.

Bob and Beverly often thought they never should have gotten married. She got pregnant when they were still in their teens, and under pressure from their parents, they married. Bob worked as a laborer in construction, and his weekend "hobby" was vegetating in front of the TV with a six-pack of beer and a bag of potato chips. Beverly was bright and energetic, and as the years went by, apart from their children, they had less and less in common.

Eventually, Beverly met a friend who was challenging and caring, and the friendship deepened into a lesbian relationship. Beverly moved out with her children and for two years she lived with her friend. Then she went for counseling and found Jesus as her Savior.

Determined to do what God wanted, she broke off the relationship with the friend and came home —something her husband also wanted. But being together again didn't change their personalities or the big discrepancy in their intellects. Arguments were bound to happen and they did, frequently. As Beverly told me about one, we worked through the same process I outlined above.

"What happened?" I asked, and she told me.

"What was your response?"

"Well, I told him he was a stupid jerk" (and a few other things that weren't any more complimentary).

"Okay. What should have been your response?"

"Well, I suppose I should have cooled off and then tried to tell him how I felt about the issue."

"What do you think you need to do to make the situation right?"

After thinking for a few minutes, she said, "I suppose I need to apologize for my attitude and what I said."

She did.

Reestablishing broken relationships is not a do-it-once-and-you're-finished-with-that-for-life kind of thing. Problems are ongoing. As we encounter them, we can work through them one by one with the same questions: What happened? How did you respond? How should you have responded? What do you need to do or say to correct the situation?

BE EMPATHETIC AND WARM IN YOUR RELATIONSHIP WITH THE PEOPLE YOU HELP

There is a difference between empathy and sympathy! Sympathy is closer to pity, while empathy means, "I care." To a degree, you hurt with your friend.

But you need to maintain some degree of distance from your friend's pain. Otherwise, if your emotions carry you away so that you lose control, both of you will need help. You will be like the person who jumps in and drowns with someone, rather than staying on the bank and pulling him or her to safety.

Does this mean that you are cold and uncaring, or that you never express emotions? Hardly. That is not at all what I am suggesting. Sometimes relating to your friend on a warm, personal basis is the best therapy you can give.

Dr. William Glasser, author of the book *Reality Therapy*, believes that if just one individual believes in another person, that individual can be the anchor to reality that keeps the other person from slipping over the precipice of irrationality. You may well be that person! Just be sure that you're strong enough not to slip over the precipice along with your friend.

Once in a while, I absolutely cannot persuade someone that he is headed for disaster. In those instances, I don't preach or pound him over the head with my entreaties. I'm simply there, and my presence as a caring, empathetic person allows him to get some of the rebellion out of his heart. Having relieved some of that emotion, he often begins to listen to reason.

Jim was like that. Having grown up in a home that adhered to strict discipline and a rather pharisaic approach to what Christians do and don't do (you don't drink, smoke, go to movies, or associate with those who do), Jim married and became quite successful in his profession. Meanwhile, he was active in his church. When middle-aged boredom set in, however, he foolishly began to experiment with some of the things he would never have touched a few years before. One thing led to another. Then one day he found himself in a situation where it suddenly hit him: "You have really played the fool." Ashamed of himself and afraid that his conduct could bring embarrassment to his family, he planned to take his life in such a way that it would appear to be an accident, so the family could collect insurance. But before he did that, he told me what he planned to do.

I couldn't have outargued him, for he was far too clever for me. But I didn't need to convince him that what he had done was foolish enough and taking his life would only bring further pain to his family; he was already convinced. He wouldn't have told me of his plan if he hadn't already abandoned it. I didn't have to help him see himself as he was; he saw himself far more clearly than I did. It wasn't necessary for me to help him discover God's will; he already knew what he needed to do. All I could do was weep with him and listen. . .and listen. And pray.

Then he had a series of long, heart-to-heart talks with his wife. He realized that his strong will, which made him successful in business, intimidated his wife. Every disagreement turned into a battle he had to win, and she became frustrated trying to express her feelings. Eventually she had stopped trying and developed a life of her own. Now, with patience and a new gentleness, they could lay the foundation for a stronger relationship between them.

He also began to renew his relationship with the Lord. This time, though, he did not base his relationship with God on the foundation of what others expected of him (especially his parents' old set of expectations), but on what God expected. His faith became deeper, more intense. He separated the wheat from the chaff and held that which was good.

Years have passed, and that struggle has long since faded into the oblivion of God's forgetfulness. This man went on to play an important part in God's work. But what he learned might have been lost had I pushed too hard to accomplish what only God could do.

DISCOVER THE POWER OF PRAYER IN EFFECTING CHANGE

Earlier in this book, I encouraged you to pray as you counsel, asking the Lord to give you insight and wisdom as you work with your friend. Praying with your friend should be just as natural and relaxed as your conversation with that person.

Sometimes I pray with a person as we begin a session of lay counseling. I may say something like, "Terry, before we get into this today, let's take a few minutes and ask the Lord to guide us." On other occasions, I'll pray with a person during the session or lead him in prayer, saying words of confession that I ask him to make his own. When there is sin that needs to be confessed, I say something like, "Look, you've told me clearly what the problem is. Let's tell the Lord what you've just told me." I'll lead in prayer briefly for a few seconds and then say, "You put it in your own words and tell the Lord just what you've told me!" Almost always there is a breaking and rending of the emotions as the confession comes out in prayer.

Prayer is a spiritual therapy through which God forgives sin and the Holy Spirit cleanses a person's conscience. It is a means of relieving tension that allows fruitful communication to follow. Prayer is also a good technique for resolving conflict, for you cannot tell the Lord how you feel about an issue while you hold hands with the person with whom you are in conflict and then hurl angry words at each other.

When I am counseling with a couple who are struggling with problems, I will often ask them to make a commitment to pray with each other for a few minutes each day, clasping hands together and letting the words flow out of their hearts. The next time we are together, I ask how prayer is affecting their relationship and problem. Almost always, I find that these prayer times are instrumental in their healing as a couple.

As a counselor-friend, you need to pray for the person you are trying to help, asking God to undertake her healing and restoration. When I pray and ask for God's help, my expectations are increased. Once I ask God to do something, I expect problems to be resolved. This makes my attitude more optimistic as I counsel—and hope is both powerful and contagious.

The power of prayer in counseling has yet to be fully appreciated and practiced, but it is one of the greatest resources available to us.

Flow with the Spirit

Writing to the Galatians, Paul cataloged the acts of the sinful nature—the problems that bring many people to us—and then contrasted the fruit of the Spirit with these. He wrote, "Those who belong to Christ Jesus have crucified the sinful nature with its passions and desires. Since we live by the Spirit, let us keep in step with the Spirit" (Galatians 5:24–25 NIV). The word Paul uses, translated "keep in step," means "march" or "follow." As counselors, we need to remember that God is the parade Leader; we are merely His followers. As you pray, utilize the Word of God, and guide your friend into the path of God's will, you are keeping in step with the Holy Spirit.

This, of course, means that you need to be filled with the Spirit, making Christ Lord of your life, allowing His Word to guide you in your personal life. As David wrote long ago, "The godly man is a good counselor because he is just and fair and knows right from wrong" (Psalm 37:30–31 TLB).

May God help you as you help others.

QUESTIONS FOR THOUGHT AND DISCUSSION

1. What would you consider to be successful counseling?

2. Are you discouraged when you watch your friends repeatedly make the same mistakes, despite your best advice? If so, what Scriptures speak to your disappointment?

3. In your own words, describe the difference between empathy and sympathy. Have you ever found yourself in a situation where you identified *too* strongly with another's pain? What was the result?

4. Why is prayer a valuable counseling technique?

5. How does being a counselor-friend challenge your own faith?

Appendix

When to Recommend Professional Help

by Dwight L. Carlson, M.D.

Dedicated and empathetic Christians have a tremendous opportunity to help the emotionally hurting and wounded in our midst. In fact, it is my belief that pastoral and lay counselors can do much of the counseling that now is being done by professionals.

It's wonderful if you choose to participate in this ministry. But it is also crucial that you recognize some of the limitations laypeople face when counseling. Without an understanding of these confines, you could actually do harm.

One such limitation is your time and patience. Helping a person who has deep-seated emotional symptoms often requires a lot of time—which the average pastor and most lay individuals don't have to give. To begin counseling a troubled person and then abruptly limit or stop the help can further injure him or her. I urge you to be aware of this possibility and to refer the person to someone who will commit to the duration of counseling.

Many psychological symptoms require the expertise of a professional. For instance, some suicidal individuals need medication to decrease their depression; they may even need the protective environment of a hospital. Likewise, the homicidal or psychotic person (one who has lost touch with reality) should have expert care. The lay counselor will be ill equipped to handle a psychotic individual's hallucinations or paranoia.

Some medical illnesses masquerade as emotional disorders. For example, abnormalities of the endocrine system, or virtually any other system of the body, can sometimes first present themselves with emotional symptoms. This should be kept in mind, as the troubled individual may need a thorough physical evaluation.

In a similar way, some emotional illnesses have a biological component, and medications can be very helpful for these disorders. Some noteworthy examples include:

1. Severe depression, especially if there is marked difficulty in functioning, or a disturbance in sleep, appetite, and other bodily functions.

2. Panic attacks, which feature an overwhelming abrupt onset of fear with physical symptoms such as heart palpitations, dizziness, etc.

3. Manic-depressive illness, in which

individuals experience periods of extreme emotional highs or euphoria followed by marked depression.

4. Psychosis or schizophrenia, in which individuals lose contact with reality.

5. Obsessive Compulsive Disorder, characterized by repetitive thoughts or behavior. Sufferers of OCD exhibit behaviors such as washing their hands many times each day or repeatedly checking that all windows and doors are locked before leaving their homes.

Be ready to help the many you can—but always be aware of your limitations, and refer your friend to a professional when appropriate.

SELECTING A THERAPIST

Just as it's very important to choose a fellowship of believers that fosters your spiritual growth, so it is equally important to select the right therapist. Here are some guidelines for a person seeking professional counseling:

First, when selecting a therapist, the recommendation of a trusted friend, pastor, or family physician is probably your best resource. If you are unable to gain direction through a personal recommendation, you may find help from some of the larger Christian organizations that compile lists of recommended therapists. For instance, Focus on the Family, of Colorado Springs, Colorado, has several individuals whose main role is to refer callers to the best therapists they can locate. Focus on the Family can be reached at (719) 531–3400.

The American Association of Christian Counselors (AACC), with headquarters in Forest, Virginia, has a list of Christian counselors. AACC can be reached by calling (800) 526–8673 or (804) 525–9470. The Christian Association for Psychological Studies (CAPS), located in New Braunfels, Texas, also maintains a list of referrals. Its telephone number is (830) 629–2277.

There are several Christian schools of psychology that may be able to give you the name of an alumnus practicing near you. They include the Fuller Theological Seminary, Graduate School of Psychology in Pasadena, California at (626) 584–5500 and Rosemead School of Psychology in La Mirada, California at (562) 903–4867.

There are also several Christian proprietary organizations that offer Christian therapy. They include New Life Ministries at (800) 545–1819 or (800) 639–5433, and Rapha Treatment Centers at (800) 383–4673.

For Christian twelve-step programs, useful in the treatment of addictions and some compulsive behavior, Overcomers' Outreach of La Habra, California at (714) 491–3000 will give you the location of a group closest to your home.

A Christian physician or dentist who is a member of the Christian Medical Dental Society (CMDS) will have access to a directory of Christian psychiatrists who are also members of CMDS.

I cannot vouch for the quality of every therapist referral you might receive from the above sources—but I believe you'll be better off using these sources than the Yellow Pages. I would be most careful of relying solely on advertising as your means of picking a therapist. Many therapists teach or give classes in churches and/or through adult education programs in your community. If you have the time to attend, these classes afford an opportunity to get to know the therapists in greater depth.

After you have obtained the name of one or several therapists—call them. Tell the therapist that you are interested in some counseling, but would like to ask a few questions before you schedule an appointment. Inquire as to whether or not it's a good time for the therapist to talk. I personally am willing to spend five or occasionally ten minutes with a person on the phone; but it's important that it not be at a time when I am under a schedule pressure.

Some of the specific questions you should ask include:

1. What is your training? How many years have you been in practice?

2. Are you a Christian? What does that mean to you? Do you utilize your Christian beliefs in your therapy? How?

3. Are there areas of counseling in which you have a special interest or training? Are there areas that you would rather let another therapist handle?

You may want to begin to address other issues as well. For example:

1. You might tell a bit about your specific problem and ask how the therapist would generally handle such a situation. Don't be afraid to ask about specific concerns. If, for instance, you are having marital problems, ask for the therapist's view on divorce. You want to be sure he or she has the same standards you believe are important.

2. It's appropriate to ask what the therapist's fees are and any questions you might have as to how insurance is handled.

3. For some individuals, the age of the therapist may be important. It is appropriate to ask this question, but be aware that

the therapist may have some questions for you, too. Personally, I like to know a little about the prospective patient, his or her problem, past treatment, and so on. Don't let those questions surprise you.

Finally, if you are comfortable with the therapist, make an appointment. After a few sessions, decide whether or not you will be able to relate freely with the therapist and if you think she or he will be able to help you. An awareness of the following items may help you to make that decision:

For the more severe illnesses or for those requiring medications, the type of training the therapist had is important. A psychiatrist is a medical doctor who has been through medical school, an internship, and at least three years of additional training in the field of psychiatry. As a medical doctor, he or she is more prone to look for the biological causes of problems and can prescribe medications when necessary. For some problems, this is very important.

All therapists go through a training period, or "internship." Even while receiving this training, they can be helpful for many problems—and are often less expensive. For the more tenacious problems, however, a seasoned therapist of at least five to ten years of experience is advisable.

If a person really needs therapy, they should seek it out. I know that cost can be a factor. But sometimes I remind people that if they had pneumonia, seldom, in our society, would they say, "I can't afford the treatment." Often family or friends will talk individuals out of getting the therapy they desperately need. Would you let a well-meaning friend talk you out of getting a chest X-ray and taking antibiotics for pneumonia? I hope not!

Counselors with a doctorate have more training and experience; and as stated earlier, there are situations where this is important. However, I know excellent therapists who are psychiatrists, psychologists, psychiatric social workers, and marriage and family therapists (MFTs). To me, what is most important is that the therapist is skilled in his or her field, is truly dedicated to Christian principles, has worked through most of his or her own areas of weakness, and has empathy—a person who is able and willing to walk with a patient through his or her emotional struggles.

NOTES

CHAPTER 1: YOU CAN HELP PEOPLE!

1. William F. Gingerich, *Shorter Lexicon of the Greek New Testament* (Chicago: The University of Chicago Press, 1965), 162.
2. "Psychiatry on the Couch," *Time,* 2 April 1979, 74.
3. "Psychoanalysis: Identity Crisis," *The Washington Post, Insight* section, and "Psychiatry on the Couch," ibid.
4. Karl Menninger, *Whatever Became of Sin?* (New York: Bantam Books, 1978), 34.

CHAPTER 2: GETTING STARTED

1. Jay Adams, *Competent to Counsel* (Grand Rapids: Baker Book House, 1970), 76.

CHAPTER 4: THE COUNSELING PROCESS

1. Frank Pittman, *Private Lies: Infidelity and the Betrayal of Intimacy* (New York: W. W. Norton and Company, 1989) quoted in "Secrets of Staying Together," *Reader's Digest,* March 1989, 152.
2. William Glasser, *Reality Therapy* (New York, N.Y.: Harper & Row, 1975), xi–xxix.
3. Pittman, 151.

CHAPTER 5: DIAGNOSE THE PROBLEM
            BUT TREAT THE WHOLE PERSON

1. Lawrence Crabb Jr., "Moving the Couch into the Church," *Christianity Today,* 22 September 1978, 17–18.
2. Ibid.
3. Ibid.

CHAPTER 6: COUNSELING "BY THE BOOK" OR BY *THE* BOOK?

1. Bernie Zilbergeld, "A Psychotherapist Looks at What's Wrong with His Profession," *The Register*, 7 August 1986, Section J.I.

2. David Holzman, *The Washington Post*, 6 December 1986, *Insight* section, 17.

3. Garth Wood as quoted by Newton Malony, "Is Neurosis for Real?" *Christianity Today*, 20 March 1987, 68.

4. John 14:16, 26; 15:26; 16:7.

5. Romans 15:16; 1 Corinthians 6:11; 2 Thessalonians 2:13.

6. Adams, 25.

7. William Kirk Kilpatrick, *Psychological Seduction* (Nashville: Thomas Nelson, 1983), 10.

8. Newton Malony, 67.

CHAPTER 7: USING THE BIBLE TO COUNSEL RELATIONSHIP PROBLEMS

1. Ted Engstrom with Robert Larson, *Integrity* (Waco: Word, 1987), 10.

2. See Beverly Caruso, *Loving Confrontation* (Minneapolis: Bethany House, 1988).

CHAPTER 8: USING THE BIBLE TO COUNSEL EMOTIONAL PROBLEMS

1. Gingerich, 96.

2. Frank Minirth and Paul Meier, *Happiness Is a Choice* (Grand Rapids, Michigan: Baker Book House, 1988).

3. Harold J. Sala, *Depression Stoppers* (Laguna Niguel, California: Guidelines Press, n.d.).

CHAPTER 9: USING THE BIBLE TO COUNSEL ADDICTIVE BEHAVIOR

1. Henry Bolsey Woolf, ed., *Webster's New Collegiate Dictionary* (Springfield, Massachusetts: Merriam-

Webster, Inc., 1979), 13.

2. Toni Grant, *Being a Woman* (New York: Random House, 1988), 51.

3. Ibid., 52.

Other Books by HAROLD SALA

Heroes: People Who Made a Difference in Our World
Today's generation needs heroes—people of substance and depth, not just celebrities. Harold Sala offers more than one hundred biographical sketches of heroic men and women—some significant, some unknown, some biblical, some historical, and some contemporary—but all worthy of emulating. Promise Press: ISBN 1-57748-378-2

    Hardback   256 pgs $14.99

Tomorrow Starts Today
Subtitled *365 Guidelines for Daily Living,* this devotional focuses on what builds you up, rather than what tears you down. Harold Sala encourages readers to look heavenward and draw their strength from God. A short Scripture passage parallels each day's main thought. Barbour Publishing: ISBN 1-57748-607-2

    Leatherette   512 pgs $4.97

ALSO AVAILABLE:

Created for a Purpose by Darlene Sala
Many women—Christian and non-Christian alike—constantly struggle with life's problems, often becoming depressed and despairing. Written specifically for women, Created for a Purpose reminds readers that God loves them completely and made them with a special purpose in mind—to create eternal beauty in them through all of life's joys and sorrows. Barbour Publishing: ISBN 1-57748-588-2

    Leatherette   224 pgs $4.97

Available wherever books are sold.
Or order from:

Barbour Publishing, Inc.
P.O. Box 719
Uhrichsville, Ohio 44683
http://www.barbourbooks.com

If you order by mail, add $2.00 to your order for shipping.
Prices are subject to change without notice.